Just Quit Already!
The Employee's Escape Plan for a Toxic Culture

TYLER KOCH

DEDICATION

For Jaclyn and Bentley- living proof of unconditional love.

CONTENTS

Preface

People may say that I have a hard time keeping a job. Who knows? When I began examining my career and why I couldn't seem to find a place that truly made me happy, I knew that the reasons for my discontent couldn't be exclusive to me. So I began putting together *Just Quit Already!* based on my previous work experiences and basically answering the question "What went wrong?" If I had a competitive compensation and benefits package and was working for an organization that had a great reputation by precedent and by practice, shouldn't that be enough? Absolutely not.

If you're an employee who is struggling to find the motivation to continue to go to work and contribute when you feel that there is something about your job that doesn't seem quite right- *Just Quit Already!* will help you pin point the root cause of your discontent. Because, after all, life's too short not to do what you love.

Just Quit Already! is designed to take you through three stages of addressing your disengagement head-on, by providing insights and anecdotes to understanding the forces at work behind the scenes that could be affecting your work-life relationship. Part One looks into your workplace in terms of behaviors and trends, as you will gain insight into uncovering the identity of the true problem. Part Two goes further into the psychology of the problematic areas as you will develop an in-depth understanding for the root causes of the negative thoughts, feelings, and behaviors. Part Three helps you digest the workplace toxicity and decide "What should I do about it?" as you'll be equipped with tools and best practices for making changes to your own behavior or taking a stand as you make a graceful exit. However, we don't stop there! We will discuss some tips and considerations for choosing a culture that is right for you as you return to work ready for an engaging and rewarding employee experience.

Just Quit Already! is your comprehensive guide to getting what you want in the workplace, after definitively declaring what you don't. Enjoy

Introduction
Both Guns Blazin'

My Mentor: "Okay…If you're telling me you're going to quit your job, then you better walk in there with both guns blazin' and not leave any questions as to why you want out!"

In today's workforce, more and more employees are finding themselves unhappy with their job or career path. The unhappiness leads to a disengaged employee and often an unhealthy personal life. The big question: When was the last time you went to bed satisfied with your day's work and excited about the job you were walking into on the next day? Can you remember talking with your friends about all of the things going well in your job, as opposed to sharing with them the seemingly ridiculous request that your boss made of you last week? Bottom line: if you spend more time dreading going to work than you do feeling inspired and excited for your next opportunity to contribute, then you may have found yourself in a company culture that can only be described with one word: *toxic* (and I don't mean that in the intriguing and seductive Britney Spears kind of way).

Fortunately, you have in your hands a book that allows you to examine your current performance and workplace contributions as well as your organizational culture in an innovative and comprehensive way. *Just Quit Already!* has been designed to provide a 360-degree review of common themes of disengaged employee performance as well as common trends in toxic leadership and company cultures. This book is for employees who know that they want out and are looking for a clear and concise road map to greater career discovery and success.

As a seasoned Human Resources professional who has worked in various facets of the contemporary workforce, ranging from the federal government, to a global for-profit corporation, to a family business, as well as a non-profit organization, I've experienced and evaluated the most toxic of organizational cultures laced with immature and inexperienced leadership. I've also seen what works well and the components of an organization that can create an engaging and rewarding employee relationship. Throughout this text, you'll see the ins and outs of working environments with which you may already be familiar, as well as gain insight into how to manage your expectations for what you truly want out of a job and career.

If you've made the decision to quit your job, congratulations- you've accomplished the hardest part! Now is the time to objectively review your organization and your contributions to discover exactly what went wrong. If you haven't quite decided that you're ready to schedule the meeting with the boss and admit to how much company time you've been using to update your resume' and search for other jobs as you finalize your departure- that's okay too! But if you're curious if *Just Quit Already!* will bring you some benefit in evaluating your career options, consider the following questions: Do you spend more time on *Pinterest* (or procrastinating in other ways) on the clock than you probably should? Do you find yourself "venting" about your coworkers, managers, and overall environment more frequently than you do sharing exciting happenings that are going on? Honestly, are you overqualified and subsequently bored (and when you talk about what you do and where you work to your friends, do you always feel the need to justify your job in some way? i.e. "It's just a stepping stone", or, "Yeah I know I don't make a lot, but the benefits are great!")? Do you see a clear path to advancement and feel motivated to pursue it given what you know about the management environment? Has your health deteriorated in some capacity since you began this job?

In one of my last positions, I made a decision to exit the organization as it had become entirely too toxic to continue my employment without doing long-term damage to my self-confidence, my health, and my reputation. The issue in this case is that I hadn't let anyone know what I was feeling until it was too late. The night before I was going to interview for a promotion, I told a mentor of mine that I couldn't do it, and I had to get out. He responded; "Okay...but if you're telling me you're going to quit, then you better walk in there with both guns blazing and not leave any questions as to why you want out!" So, that's what I did. I walked into the Board of Directors meeting and dropped a verbal pipe-bomb of anger, disdain, and disgust with the current state of the organization and what had become of its leadership. This was a purely emotional response to the stresses of the toxic culture that I found myself in and was completely the wrong way to leave an organization.

Don't be the employee who waits until he's physically, mentally, and emotionally drained before he has to explode his way out of the company. Be the employee who takes the time to examine his actions and contributions and has the moral courage to declare "Maybe I'm the problem!" Be the employee who can objectively look at the organization and provide specific examples of where poor leadership and a lack of values-based management are breeding toxicity in the workplace and say "It's not me - it's you. Working here longer than another two weeks doesn't support what I want out of my life and career, and for that reason- I'm out." Be the employee who doesn't wait until it's too late to address his workplace concerns when he realizes the negative effects that his job is having on other aspects of his life. Step up and decide to quit settling for less than you deserve.

The principles and practices that you're about to read have all been proven to generate positive work-life balances and rewarding employee experiences. All you have to do is commit to gaining control of your career and staying focused through the end. Each chapter will present you with a new concept for your creation of a more self-aware and empowered employee as you strive to finish this book gaining more tools for your productive employee toolbox.

Your career belongs to you and you alone; not your boss, not the board of directors, and not the company- regardless of how they've made you feel up until this point. Take control, commit to yourself to expect more out of a job, and **JUST QUIT ALREADY!**

Chapter One
Well, Here You Are.

Take Home Message

• Failing to meet your cultural expectations; poor job fit; little or no performance feedback; a cloudy environment with no chance of career growth; little feeling of value, high stress; diminished trust; and cultural toxicity are likely among the top reasons you want to quit

• Employees come to the workplace with four basic needs: Trust, Utility, Recognition, Value. Lacking one or more can lead to disengagement and departure

• The "indiscriminant applicant," the employee on a "search for affirmation," those "testing the waters," and those screaming that they "Gotta get out" are generally those looking to quit

---

Milton: And I said, I don't care if they lay me off either, because I told, I told Bill that if they move my desk one more time, then, then I'm quitting, I'm going to quit. And, and I told Don too because they've moved my desk four times already this year, and I used to be over by the window, and I could see the squirrels, and they were married... But then, they switched from the Swingline to the Boston stapler, but I kept my Swingline stapler because it didn't bind up as much, and I kept the staples for the Swingline stapler and it's not okay because if they take my stapler then I'll, I'll, I'll set the building on fire...

-Stephen Root as Milton
Waddams, Office Space

You finally decided, whether it's been two days, two weeks, two years, or two decades - you've decided to say those two words (I'm referring to "I quit"; don't get carried away) to your employer and walk out the door. That's right. It's time to quit. You've had enough. You've done your time. You created some results or maybe you haven't, but at the end of the day, you're ready to go- and it is now time to let everybody know. While we'll talk about how exactly to do that later, right now, let's talk about what's gotten you to this point.

Your life cycle as an employee with the organization you've decided to leave is probably one that has all begun the same way. You probably started with some level of excitement and enthusiasm about this next journey in your career. You probably remember walking through the door and having your first conversation with HR (assuming you had an actual HR department. The last organization that I worked with, I filled out all my paperwork to include the I-9 at home, sent it all in via fax, and then just showed up and began to contribute on day one). Yet, somewhere over the course of your career, of your time with the organization, you began to question that decision. The enthusiasm began to fade. The excitement wasn't quite there. That feeling that led you through the door in this first instance was almost unrecognizable as you dreaded walking through the same door at this point- and that's when you began toying with the idea of leaving.

What was it that finally pushed you over the edge? Did you ever really fit in? Were you satisfied with the culture of the workplace when compared to the promises of the hiring process? What was it that caused you to make that transition between, "I'm happy here producing.", and "I'm ready to get out as fast as I possibly can!"? Some of the things that people talk about when they discuss leaving their careers simply boil down to eight common characteristics.

Eight Reasons You Want Out

First, maybe the job or the work environment was not what you expected. Maybe everything you read in the reviews from other employees (i.e. Glassdoor), or everything that you heard from insiders when you were on the outside, and everything you'd seen on blog sites and social media as far as the image the organization was projecting was nothing more than a façade. It's possible that as soon as you settled into your office and your desk that you found out that the people, the environment, and the leadership/managerial culture was not exactly what you were hoping for. The organization may not even do what you anticipated they did. There are a variety of reasons that can contribute to the disappointment following the initial discovery that the company you thought you worked for only bears a mere resemblance to the organization to which you are actually contributing. Often, the disappointment can be rooted in the concept of "expectation management," and how diligent you were in finding out everything about the organization before signing the offer letter. Getting a job offer is much like buying a car or a house: it's quite an emotional experience. Your personal satisfaction in receiving the affirmation that a company has selected you above all others may often blur your objectivity in doing your homework on the organization. So, if the actual culture doesn't match the predicted experience, then reflect on what efforts you contributed in the beginning of the employer/employee relationship?

Second, maybe the job itself doesn't fit the skill set you're bringing to the table. Employees often find themselves realizing that the "other duties as assigned" bullet point on their job descriptions are predominantly what they do, leaving them feeling that their talents aren't being utilized to their fullest potential. This is often a sign of poor organizational development strategy, as the organization is simply not robust enough to have employees simply focus on their "primary" job requirements; therefore, they find themselves picking up "other duties", albeit assigned more often that they'd like.

Third, maybe there's too little-to-no feedback in your job performance. The manager may possess the "once a year" (as indicated by company policy) mentality that so many people from the baby boomer generation are accustomed to. This is quite understandably a disheartening environment for employees, especially when they don't find out until it's too late that they're walking into a board meeting for an annual performance review only to discover that management has been unhappy with what they've produced. Generationally, employees are developing an expectation for more frequent feedback. But, if you're not part of an organization that supports that expectation, then it can be frustrating! I mean, people give feedback for a "taking my dog to the vet" Facebook status update!

Fourth, the company climate can be described as "cloudy with no chance of career growth." There is no next level or plan for your professional growth and development. If an employee isn't able to see a clear path to something greater, his innate ability to pursue accomplishment will be diminished, and disengagement will follow. Employees who have graduated high school and beyond are conditioned to a system of advancement after relatively predictable intervals, so an all-of-a-sudden lack of movement vertically or otherwise feels unnatural. You as an employee may believe that the manager's job is to "hold the ladder" in order to stabilize your upward movement in the organization when the reality is that there's no ladder put in place for you to climb.

Fifth, maybe you don't feel that you're creating any value to the workplace. Are you recognized at all for your contributions? Are others recognized when you don't seem to be? If you're not feeling any appreciation for what you do, then that may transcend into the overall perception of your total value in the organization. If you're not valued where you are, then the natural thought is to go down a path towards a place where you will feel more appreciated.

What is your gut reaction when you read these questions:
- Are you overworked?
- Are you stressed out more often than you're relaxed?

The sixth reason that people leave their jobs is because they feel that they've given too much of themselves to the organization and not received enough in return. Stress can manifest itself in many ways, and you don't have to look very far in your personal and professional life to find areas that have been damaged as the result of a stressful environment. Economic hardships, bad hiring decisions, immature leadership, etc... can all create more work for you if you're the type of employee who likes to ensure that you do everything you can to make certain that the organization keeps moving forward, *even if that means doing other people's jobs.*

Here is one concept that will severely limit the efforts of leadership in any organization if compromised: trust. Honestly ask yourself, "Do I have any trust in my leaders?" If there's none, then that's the key decision for most people to walk out the door. But, as deadly as a lack of trust can be for leaders, it can be more detrimental if there's no trust and confidence between employees and their coworkers. After all, most employees interact with their leader/manager on an occasional basis, whereas the interaction with coworkers is more frequent and by many degrees more influential when shaping the employees' emotional perspective of the organization. Do you often find yourself questioning hiring decisions? Do you wonder how someone else was given a promotion and you weren't? Do you wonder why someone was hired (or even rehired) into the organization when they seemingly don't contribute half as much as you do? Questioning these types of decisions are key indicators of waning trust in the decision-making within your organization.

At the end of the day, the primary reason that people leave can be summed up in two words: *toxic culture.* It's going to sound weird, but do you feel guilty (or even a little dirty) about the work you've contributed to the organization? Everything you once believed about the job you have can be shattered by some of the elements in this list. Are the values and culture of your workplace reflective of your personal values, and do they genuinely deliver personal satisfaction and pride in what you do? It's never easy when an employee realizes that he's not where he thought he'd be in his career for one reason or another. Fortunately, the first step is admitting there is a problem- now, we can get to some root causes.

What You're Looking for in a (professional) Relationship

There are really four basic needs that an employee looks for in any work place. From the first job you have as a teenager trying to make a few bucks to your growth into a lifelong career employee that's providing for a family and saving for retirement, the four components you will consistently need to feel and experience in the work place are

- Trust

- Utility

- Recognition

- Value

Trust

First and foremost, employees need to feel trusted. From managers, board members, colleagues, and subordinates, trust is key. When I worked for a family business a little while ago, (spoiler alert: I'll tell you the story of that a little bit later) it touted having five core values: honesty, integrity, teamwork, trust, and love. I eventually quit. They understood the need for having those values not only in place but also upheld in order to thrive as an organization. As a business that was built on the backs of a relationship with the customer, (the primary revenue was generated from the sale of a product) the commitment to maintaining an unwavering reliability in all transactions, all of the time, was of the utmost importance. Granted, there were times when customers or employees could point to and say that they experienced a weakening in the trust of their relationship with this business for one reason or another, but they could do so with the confidence that their assertion would be met with the organizational effort to regain that trust at all costs. It was always clear that trust was felt in all interactions all the time.

As members of the human race, we're innately attracted to those who demonstrate the same values and beliefs that we do. We're attracted to cultures and environments where our values and beliefs align. When we hold the same beliefs and see that alignment, trust emerges. This trust is what allows us to leave our families on a daily basis and go to a workplace where we feel like we're going to be supported; we trust that the workplace, the environment, and the people that we're going to spend our time with believe in the same concepts and ideals that we do. We trust that the organization ultimately wants us to return to our families more profitable and in a better position professionally than when we left them.

In order for employees and organizations to find passion and profitability (as well as bring those two concepts together to create a legacy), trust must exist across all organizational levels, which begins with ensuring *values alignment*. In considering passion and profitability, consider a few the most successful individuals that you can think of in business and otherwise. Look at the Warren Buffets, Steve Jobs, Alan Mulallys, and it won't take very long of searching to find evidence of what they'll tell you they believe in. You'll find reviews of those who have worked alongside them repeatedly filled with the word *trust* among other values. The start-with-the-why philosophy not only has led them to develop great organizations, but their peers and colleagues would consider the most iconic leaders to be great employees. They create companies where people want to work because they understand why it's important to have engaged employees who believe in the organizational mission.

Utility

The second aspect that employees need to experience is a feeling of utility. They need to feel like when they come to work, they contribute to something greater than themselves, and that they're using all of their strengths, talents, and skill sets to improve the bottom line. An employee's job should be challenging because he is required to produce at an intellectually stimulating level-not necessarily a physically exhausting one. With a desire to improve their working environment (team, department, etc.), and to improve the results of their job responsibilities, employees will need to be challenged to produce and experience the feeling of being useful. It sounds so simple, yet this concept has become so uncommon.

Recognition

Third is recognition. Now, there are multiple articles and texts and academic resources to tell you what an employee needs in terms of personal recognition. There's the five love languages that have actually been translated into "The 5 Languages of Appreciation in the Workplace" (Words of Affirmation, Quality Time, Acts of Service, Tangible Gifts, Physical Touch) that tell you how to recognize each other as coworkers, as well as recognize your bosses; moreover, it informs managers how to recognize their employees. The fact is that regardless of the degree, everyone wants/needs to be recognized on some level; the challenge will be knowing your coworkers well enough to recognize them in the way that they view as personal and valuable.

Value

Fourth is value. Employees need to understand that they matter not only to the team members but to the leadership structure as well. Value is demonstrated differently to every team member, but the conscious effort by leadership to understand exactly how the efforts of each employee contribute to the overall organizational strategy and providing the feedback to the employee validating their work will remind them that they are *in fact* making a difference. Leadership and management taking the time to share the vision for the future of the company, sharing financial conditions when possible, and simply asking (and listening) for input on strategic decisions from the individual employees will serve as affirmation that their contributions are worthwhile. Engaged leadership and willing employees who take the time to discover what makes each team member "get out of bed in the morning,"-will provide insight for structuring a values-aligned work relationship between the organization and its employee base. Employees need to believe that what truly matters to them is valued by the organization in terms of their efforts and results.

But What About the Money?

When surveyed, many managers say that the primary reason their employees are leaving their jobs is somehow related to compensation. Another organization must have made them a better offer (surprisingly out of the blue) that's led them to pursue making greater compensation with better benefits. The reality is actually inversely proportional in terms of employees who actually pursue more money when compared to those who actually leave due to gaps in some of the needs that we referenced above, and one or several of their four basic needs are not being met in their current workplace; therefore, they've moved into a category of employees referred to as "disengaged". The *Gallup* organization conducted a 2015 survey regarding the levels of engagement among employees. Here's the bottom line: Engaged employees will stay and disengaged employees will consider leaving. *Gallup* indicates that roughly 60% of employees in the workforce right now are disengaged on some level. They're either disinterested, moving toward disengaged, or actively disengaged and moving toward destructive "I'm-out of-here" behavior.

Your Situational Awareness

Now, where you are in terms of your personal employee engagement is a valid question to answer, but the deeper cause is getting into why. When diving into the root causes of your disengagement, begin with an examination of the four basic needs of an employee and determine where your organization may be falling short. Do you feel an overarching sense of trust all of the time in all interactions? Do you show up every day expecting to perform to the full extent of your abilities? Do you see a return on your efforts in terms of value to the organization and the management hierarchy? Lastly, when your efforts create results, does your organization respond with genuine recognition?

Toxic or Non Toxic Culture- An Employee Relations Mindset

Although there will be an entire chapter dedicated to dissecting the elements of your organization, let's talk about your company culture for a minute. There are really two categories when it comes to deciphering what type of culture and organization your company exhibits: Toxic or Non Toxic. Within the toxic category, there exist two organizational mindsets when considering employee value. There is either a retention mindset, in that the organization contends: "we will do everything we possibly can to create and environment and a culture that makes this employee want to come to work and contribute every day," or there is a replacement mindset, where the company admits "We firmly believe that turnovers are going to happen, employees are going to leave, there's going to be better offers out there, and we have no choice but to expect that and anticipate that cost when we're running a line-item budget."

Determining whether your organization has a retention mindset versus replacement mindset may clear up relatively quickly why you're feeling a lack of utility or value in your current position. I would imagine that all of you who are reading this text have found that you are working as part of an organization that has the replacement mindset, at least to some degree and you realize that management may expect you walk out the door at some point (as a normal cost of doing business). When that expectation is realized, it's likely that you'll experience an immediate degradation of trust.

Fortune online conducts an annual survey cataloguing the greatest companies to work for according to their employees. Within that survey, they found that those listed as the greatest places to work experienced a 133% growth rate in their overall organizational footprint when compared to those within the same industry who were not on the list, who only marginally achieved a 25% growth. Which employee-relations mindset would you guess the "greatest" companies possessed?

Employers in organizations that have the retention mindset have experienced exponentially larger growth across multiple metrics than those who are seemingly content with turnover and replacement. Your organization, that has obviously determined you are a replaceable asset, is going to find out very quickly after you deliver those two words, "I quit" that there are unanticipated costs associated with your departure, inhibiting their operational efficiency and ability to grow. The staff that surrounded you is going to pick up more work in order to continue its daily processes, causing a net decrease in overall individual productivity. Their customer service, if that's the business that they're in, is going to experience some disruption. There's going to be some unhappy reviews (we're in a reputation economy after all) that are associated with your departure, unless they've already got a plan in place to cover the gap. It will cost money to begin the HR employee-relations cycle, as advertisement, recruitment, and onboarding will all have associated expenditures. Productivity will also find disruption across the company as people start to ask the natural question, "Why did this individual leave?", and "What lead to his departure?". The organization's ability to have real conversations with their employees about circumstances following an employee's resignation will determine whether they retain or replace more than you.

Back on the Market

If you're like most Americans, then you're not at a point where you can simply leave a job without having a backup plan in place. While you were currently contributing to one organization, you began to patrol the multiple sites that have made it so easy for applicants to move from one job to another, so you sent out some applications. You updated your resume (probably at work), and you started to search. At some point, you may have even interviewed and already have an offer letter in your hands; however, when thinking about the job market you'll be re-entering, it's important to consider the employees currently making up the applicant pool that you'll be competing against. Aside from the "High- demand, low-supply" skilled and professional labor who are offered insane amounts of money in an unpredictable economy, there are generally four types of employees who are looking to quit their jobs in pursuit of something else or at least are saturating the job market with their application materials.

First, there is the "indiscriminant applicant". These are the people who can flood a job posting from "0 applicants" to "This job has over 256 applicants" in the span of about five minutes. The indiscriminant applicant is the employee who is always looking for something else. He may not really want to leave his jobs due to some gross organizational flaw, but he simply enjoys looking at other opportunities that have emerged since he took this job. Given the increased utilization of social media by many job posters and Human Resource (HR) departments, it has become increasingly easy for employees to do a "one-click apply" type application just to see what happens. From an HR perspective, not only does this flood the job market with excess noise, but it also dampens productivity in the hiring process and causes qualified candidates to become overlooked due to the "just-get-someone-in-here" feeling that comes after a seemingly long delay. No longer do employees have to schedule time off to fish around for other opportunities (to include the time it formerly required to update and copy resumes, search the classified ads, and drive to each prospective employer). The tedious process that formerly required the use of a vacation day can now be completed while sitting in a meeting and hearing something disagreeable such as "Oh really? I'm working President's day? Nope" (cue one-click *apply*). Realistically, there are employees who will never stop applying for jobs for the entire time they're at an organization; it's just a product of the digitally-connected environment in which they live and work.

The second category of employee is the one on a "search for affirmation". After a period of time in a new position or with a new organization, employees may begin to feel disheartened about the work they are doing. Maybe it's a lack of the challenge they were hoping for or the settling in of a new boss or culture, but the employee isn't feeling the value they need from the organization. So, they begin to search for it somewhere else! This employee doesn't necessarily plan on leaving and may never disclose that he would even looked for another job; he just needs to know that he "still has it". It's a great feeling for an employee to feel the affirmation of receiving a job offer, especially if it's one that immediately incites enthusiasm and an increased level of self-confidence. If an employee has been sucked into an environment that is paying him appropriately for the work he does, but he knows he can do more, then it's not uncommon for him to seek out different opportunities to remind himself that he's valuable to someone. It's the employee giving himself a reminder that "Hey, I could leave if I wanted to. I know you want me here, but someone else wants me too because I'm that good."

Unlike the indiscriminant applicant, the employee on a search for affirmation will actually go through the hiring process and pursue an offer, although he will wait until the proposal has been made to respectfully decline. This is not the kind of offer that employees will use for negotiation in pursuit of higher compensation because it wasn't rooted in true discontent rather just annoyance more than anything. When an employee returns from having gone through this process, he may have a renewed sense of self-worth and a bolder sense of assertion; after all, he knows now that if he wanted to leave…he can.

I went through this scenario with one of my previous positions. I was getting extremely bored in what I was doing (and what I was *not* doing), so I began to work my network and arrange for an interview. I spent the money to travel to the company headquarters and interview with a few people, never fully committed actually to departing my current organization. I just needed to be reminded that I was an attractive asset to an organization that wanted me to contribute. I remember driving back to my job and reflecting on the interview and then seeing the offer come through electronically. I read through it with a sense of accomplishment and then deleted it. I did decide to share with my boss that I had gone through the interview process and had received an offer, but I did so as a segue to saying that I wanted more of a challenge. I didn't leverage it for money or bonuses, but knowing that I wasn't going to take it; I used it as an opportunity for a conversation starter about what I wanted in my career. **Note:** Only employ this tactic if you're confident you've got the relationship with your boss to do so! Some may find it offensive and even dishonest if you haven't been forthright with where you've spent your time.

Category three focuses on the employees who certainly have some time in the organization and who are "testing the waters" of the job market as they seriously consider a departure. These employees are often significantly beneficial to the organization in terms of their responsibility. They've got some tenure and probably perform well in their jobs, but they are becoming increasingly disenchanted with the organization for one reason or another. They slowly began to update their resumes and started to browse job boards and career websites. In addition, they have taken an increased interest in benefits administration in COBRA protocols and begun to separate from previously-routine company practices or opportunities. The employee has made the decision that the current organization has transitioned from a potential home to a career and further to "just a job", and they're prepared to start what's next. Odds are that they've been disappointed by some facet of the company's operation or culture and no longer wish to associate or contribute to the degree they previously intended. It's not a cultural emergency, however, as the employee isn't advertising that he can no longer function in this organization for one more hour and will walk whether he has another offer or not, so he won't leave for just *any* job. This time, the employee focuses on finding the *right* job. Whether it will ever be realized or not, the employee is still determined to find the perfect home for a career - it's just not here and just not now.

Lastly, there is the employee who simply has "Gotta get out". The employee has likely been looking for a job for quite some time, as such feelings of angst don't just suddenly emerge. Regardless of what comes next, he has reached a point that he will no longer contribute any time or talent to the organization and will exit as abruptly as possible.

It's possible that this behavior could have been circumvented at some point if there were a structure in place designed to recognize it, but then the employee feels that the entire organization has turned against him, and to stay one-second longer would be a complete disregard for his personal values and self-worth. This employee has probably internalized a great deal of anger (maybe jealousy), a declining feeling of value, and has convinced himself (granted he may certainly be correct) that the organization has become unethical, unstable, and simply unbearable.

These employees can be the most damaging to the organization, as they will probably not be the first ones to volunteer their time for a smooth transition or provide ample notice (if any). The organizational responsibility to create a culture of awareness and multi-tiered communication will be the best offense to pit against this potentially detrimental cultural reflection.

Let's Do This Thing

If you've still committed to dropping those two words, "I quit," signing that final letter, packing up your office, and walking out the door, then **congratulations**: you've taken the first step! But before you make that final move, throughout the rest of *Just Quit Already!*, we're going to discuss in greater detail the reasons that employees leave. We're going to examine with surgical precision the elements of toxic culture in an organization: what that looks like, how to recognize it, and how to prevent getting back into another unsuccessful and unproductive and unhealthy employer-employee relationship. Oh yeah, we're definitely going to talk about *you*, too.

Chapter Two
Quit Projecting & Start Delivering!

Take Home Message:

- Employees can fall into a "negativity cycle" starting with negative thoughts, feelings, behaviors, and ultimate disengagement

- If you're caught in the negativity cycle, then determine at which point it began, assess the damage, and begin an action plan to leave your job

- Employees can be aggressive or passive when it comes to negative behaviors with varying degrees of damaging behavior; awareness is the first step to repair

"It's not you, it's me.... You're giving me the 'It's not you, it's me' routine? I invented 'It's not you, it's me.' Nobody tells me it's them, not me. If it's anybody, it's me."

"Alright, George, it's you."

"You're damn right it's me."

"Look, I was just trying to...."

"I know what you were trying to do. Nobody does it better than me."

"Well I'm sure you do it very well."

"Yes, well, unfortunately you'll never get the chance to find out."

- George and Gwen, breaking up, in Seinfeld's "The Lip Reader"

One of my former bosses was a big fan of *Seinfeld*; and when I say *big*, I mean **huge**. It didn't matter whether you'd seen an episode or not; if there were a *Seinfeld* reference even remotely relevant to the current topic of conversation, it was made, explained, shared on

YouTube, and then expected to be understood the next time it came up.

I never really got into *Seinfeld* outside of the few references I was expected to appreciate, but there's one segment that I think applies to those of us who have become disgruntled in our work environment. The scene above between George and Gwen as they're going back and forth about the use of the reasoning, "It's not you, it's me", resembles a common internal conflict many unhappy couples/workers struggle with in determining the source of their discontent. The bottom line: To find happiness in the workplace-you've got to stop projecting negativity; and only when that cycle of negativity is broken will you truly become a self-aware employee and an effective team member. So, before we go any further, it's time to say (out loud if you need to - whatever it takes for you to believe it) "Maybe *I'm* the problem." There can be several root causes to the toxicity in the environment that has caused you to want to get out, so we'll start with examining the one that you have the most control over: yourself.

One of the first signs of a disengaged, disgruntled employee is this aura of negativity that seems to surround every word, product, and piece of correspondence that he has produced within the workplace. The employee falls into what's known as a negativity cycle. If you search for that, you'll find a thousand (literally) different images that people have put together capturing their interpretation of this cycle, which corresponds to what employees or people in general experience when they're in an unhappy, disengaged, and depressed portion of their lives. The cycle can be pretty vicious in the workplace for not only the individual but also for others, as some of you are already aware.

The Four Phases of the Negativity Cycle

The first segment spotlights negative thoughts. When you start to think about things that upset you or things that you would (or should) have done differently, or you start to question the decisions of leaders that are above you, then the negative thinking begins.

Negative thinking becomes dangerous because it leads to negative feelings. The feelings are what will keep you up at night. You can't close your eyes without thinking about that negative experience you had in the workplace, and you begin to replay how things may have gone if you responded differently to that negativity. More often than not, one negative thought will lead to another, and that thought to yet another, etc., until you've wasted hours thinking about all of the poor decisions you've made and feeling terrible about them.

Feelings, as the emotional manifestation of negative thoughts, serve as the catalyst for negative and destructive actions. Negative actions occur when the employees move from simply being disengaged or disgruntled to being professionally destructive. Following the negative actions are decreased productivity, overall waste, job dissatisfaction, unhappy coworkers, unhappy supervisors, and especially if you're in a management position, unhappy subordinates. This is when people notice there's a problem; in other words, when it's visibly taking a toll on their ability to create results on the job.

The Employee Negativity Cycle

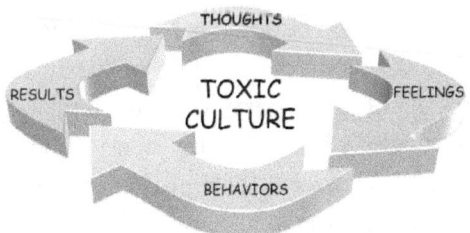

Where are you in the negativity cycle?

The first step to breaking the negativity cycle is looking at where you are right now and assessing the severity of the situation. Are you just thinking about circumstances that make you unhappy? Are they starting to creep into your personal life and affect how you are around other people who have nothing to do with your job, or are you showing signs of negative behavior within the workplace and even off the clock? Are you producing at the level that makes you happy, or do you feel that in your heart, if in a different environment, you could do more?

In pursuit of achieving negativity awareness and breaking the negativity cycle, here are some considerations to help you determine where in the cycle you fall.

When a new decision is announced or handed down from the board of directors or managers, what is your first thought? Do you consider all of the ways that it will help the organization, or do you focus on what will be difficult about its implementation?

If you find that you're a person who immediately points out the flaws in said plan, then ask yourself why. One of my longtime mentors and first managers was the type that met every proposal with what seemed like a full-frontal assault on the concept. He always found a way to question every detail of a new idea with a painstaking degree of examination, which wasn't necessarily a bad approach entirely because some people are analytical by nature; that's just how they operate; However, if you are normally an employee who is excited to challenge the conventional ways of doing business in the spirit of progress, and you suddenly begin to see anything new as an inconvenience, then a negative paradigm shift has occurred. You may have even begun to believe the mentality that the only way to carry out a plan is if it's 100% correct 100% of the time or perfect (according to your supervisor) in all aspects. Now, if that's the person that you believe you are, then think about the energy in the room when you provide your feedback in a team setting: your words may be like a vacuum that sucks all of the good, positive, creative energy out (cue *SNL*'s "Debbie Downer" theme). This theory of overgeneralization in the spirit of perfection can become more detrimental when it shifts from a project mindset to a people mindset, in the sense of labeling when it comes to your coworkers, your peers or the organization. If you can project a single negative event all of a sudden, in your perspective, then it's a broader representation of what the organization has become.

For instance, an overgeneralization about a coworker who distributes a meeting agenda with a typographical error regarding the date of the next meeting might be that this individual is not a contributor and, therefore, isn't performing to organizational standards, which in turn has officially become a detriment to the organization. This train of thought is relatively routine when you're experiencing behaviors that are a byproduct of the toxic influences and their subsequent negative feelings. I think we realize that the reasoning behind this thought process is rooted deeper than the typo on the agenda. The negative behavior is a cultural reflection, and a toxic projection. When you realize you're in the middle of the negativity cycle and begin to project your cultural discomfort, then you'll also probably notice that you're wasting valuable time and energy.

I remember when I was at one of my most dissatisfied points with one of my previous employers. The negativity became so prevalent that I couldn't do anything productive without thinking about the anticipated reception of my product by others and my subsequent reaction (not to mention how many times I misunderstood the intention of an email due to the punctuation or capitalization use by the sender). In one instance in particular, I received an email from a coworker very simply asking me a question about reserving a certain aspect of a leadership development conference that we were hosting. I was the project manager for all things curriculum and delivery that affected this particular conference, and this other individual was the liaison between the attendees and the organization. She sent me an email basically asking if a reservation had been made finalizing the facility. I took that immediately as a personal affront that this employee was passive-aggressively implying that I had apparently missed a detail, and that something that I was responsible for wasn't done. For a coworker to make that assessment and send that type of correspondence my way was highly irresponsible and unprofessional (according to me).

I sat on it for about five minutes, then immediately sent an email to my boss asking him to reprimand this employee immediately and remind her of her job responsibilities. I was technically on my day "off" when I received this, and it effectively ruined my afternoon as the negativity cycle seeped into my personal life bit by bit, as I couldn't just simply quit thinking about it. My bad mood ruined an entire trip to Bed Bath and Beyond. There lies part of the problem with email: the context was assumed one way by me but entirely intended in another way by the individual sending it. As my boss shared with me, they were developing a formal invitation to send out as a reminder that the event was coming up and were looking for one detail that I had yet to provide. *Oops.* Because of my immediate assumption that everything that I was doing was wrong, my negative reaction and poor decision making wasted not only my time but also the time of my coworker and my supervisor. The entire episode cost about 18 hours of back-and-forth communication and correspondence that could have been prevented with an assessment and correction to my own negative behavior.

Also, as it turns out, when your boss sends an email that states: "WHERE WILL YOU BE ON FRIDAY?", he just may not realize that the "Caps Lock" is on. Therefore, you don't have to write a two-paragraph response on how you're being gone on Friday is in accordance with the company's leave policy as described in the employee handbook. Not only do e-mail senders overestimate their ability to communicate feelings, but e-mail recipients also overestimate their ability to correctly decode those feelings. When you couple that with pre-existing negative thoughts, feelings, and behaviors, you waste too much time and emotion combating conflict that may not even exist (except in your own mind).

In addition to the time you'll find yourself wasting, negativity is also known for diminishing creativity and innovation. One quote that we used as a motivator in one of my previous workplaces was "innovate or die." Those who fail to innovate, fail to produce. Those who fail to produce, fail to be relevant and fail to exist. Negativity kills creativity because a negative-minded employee tends to want to come in, do the bare minimum to produce, and then simply walk away.

The engaged employee in the creative mindset wants to give what's known as "discretionary effort" to the organization, asking questions like: "What else can we do to move forward?" and "How else can we contribute?".

FYI

Discretionary Effort: *the level of effort employees could give if they wanted to, but above and beyond the minimum required. Many organizations manage performance in such a way that motivates employees to do only enough to get by, and avoid getting in trouble (negative reinforcement). Discretionary Effort is one of the most contemporary metrics in measuring employee engagement.*

Self-Assessment: Connection through Reflection

Of course, one of the first things a negative employee is going to believe in his own self- assessment is "It's not my fault" (maybe you're thinking it right now). This is where a positive relationship with a supervisor, manager, or mentor will come in handy, as they can initiate a dialogue that allows you to get to the root cause of your unhappiness, and that's exactly what we should be doing right now in order to correct course.

Think about this: Your behaviors impact the way your co-workers and boss interact with you. How would they define your behavior right now? Would they say that you're productive? Will they say that they enjoy working with you? Will they say that you're a creative person to have on the team? Do they consider you a part of the team at all? Are you a team unifier or a company divider? Now, transition to your boss. Does your boss enjoy interacting with you on a daily basis? Does he/she feel when they ask you a question that he's opening the door for this overall projection of everything that's wrong with the organization? If you're in a management position, do your subordinates enjoy taking direction from you? When they approach you, are they met with irritation like you've got so many more important things to do other than converse with them? If you put yourself in their shoes for a moment and think about how they assess your interactions, then you'll begin to understand the way your behaviors are perceived and the effect they're having in and around your office. This is one of the first steps in the assessment of your stage in the negativity cycle. In reflecting on where you are in the negativity cycle, consider your current level of workplace satisfaction. When the negativity cycle is moving in full effect, your ability to fully contribute is certainly hindered, which you'll find is directly proportional to your satisfaction. Remember the four basic needs of the employee: *Trust, Utility, Recognition,* and *Value* and ask "Is my own negativity affecting my need to be fully utilized?"

Degrees of Negativity

Of course, there are varying degrees of negative behavior demonstrated in the workplace. Imagine a spectrum of negativity with an aggressive end and a passive end. Utilizing military terminology to describe some of the personalities, the most far-right end of the aggressive behaviors would be "the general". The general is the one who criticizes and commands everyone. They're argumentative on most accounts, believe that there's only one way to do carry out procedures, and only one way to show anger. They believe that with anger comes authority, and authority leads to control. Control, in their mind, leads to progress. In terms of the workspace behavior, the general is the one who feels that he needs to call all the shots. Unlike a military general who carries an international sign of respect and accomplishment for obtaining the prestigious level of leadership, the aggressive workplace general is a title obtained through self-promotion and position alone.

The second type of individual along that spectrum is the "demolition man." This is the person who resembles the "Anger" emotion from the movie *Inside Out.* Demolition men are the ones who have temper tantrums and uncontrollable outbursts (I characterize them all sounding like Lewis Black when speaking about anything and everything). They're the ones who get loud quickly. They're what would dominate the baby boomer generation's idea of a "manager." Fortunately, this type of behavior is declining throughout United States workplaces, but it is still seen to some degree. I can tell you that in the United States military this behavior is often very effective because you put people out of their comfort zones and follow up with an immediate rebuilding of knowledge and skill. It's what you intend to do with this behavior when you immediately want to incite a response; however, if overused, then it becomes ineffective as it becomes routine behavior. In the workplace, especially one as heavy and controlled like human resources policies and behaviors and operating procedures for how to conduct one's self, it's not often found as a characteristic of an effective leader; however, effective vs. ineffective is not the conversation as the question is whether or not this behavior exists and if you can recognize it as part of the negativity cycle.

The third is the self-proclaimed "medal of honor" winner: the one who always wants to feel like the hero. He wants the credit. He wants the recognition, and he's telling you right upfront what his language of appreciation is in the workplace. However, the need to stand on that platform, especially when there's not a clear promotion track, is one that often is a keystone example of the negative, disgruntled, disengaged employee. This is the employee who wants to take credit in a public setting to remind himself, to some degree, that he is valued. If he's not getting the value and appreciation shown by other areas of the workplace, he's going to make absolutely sure that he gets it in one way or another himself. That's what the grandstanding is all about.

The fourth characteristic, and this is transitioning a little bit into the passive state of negativity is where you have the sniper. The sniper is the one who will do most of the talking behind your back and quietly criticize. They're the ones who will volunteer to a lot of promises within a staff meeting or board meeting but very rarely actually delivers. They'll tell a good story, but back it up with few results. They're the ones who will always have an opinion but seldom have a solution. The snipers are often times the most difficult to root out because they're not always contributing unless it's in one of those meeting settings. However, don't be fooled by their confidence in making statements. Generally, somewhere deep down, they're unhappy with the workplace; otherwise, they would be producing the results to validate those opinions and assertions.

The fifth, and most passively negative employee, is the one with the "dropped pack"- meaning that they don't even bother pretending that they're trying to contribute anymore. They'll show up physically, but are mentally showing signs of being completely checked-out of the organization. They may not be overly critical in conversation but could best be described as "complacent", where they appear to be serving some function, but to what degree they're effective is undetermined. The complacent employees are just going through the motions of contribution, and their mere presence is discouraging to the above-average producer.

These behaviors and five types of negative personalities along the spectrum do not comprise an all -inclusive list, so it's quite possible that you're already thinking of more examples and behavior patterns to add. The question that you should be asking yourself right now is "Where do I align?". Maybe it's not one of those five that we outlined, or maybe it's somewhere in between. Maybe it's considerably further down the list of the spectrum on the passive side where your manager or coworkers don't consider you a contributor at all. That is the worst place to be because it's highly likely that this lack of value and utility are drastically increasing your negative behaviors.

If you've reached the point of the negativity cycle where your behaviors are such that you just have no interest in having a contribution of any sort, no grandstanding, no opinions, no sniping, no medal of honor winner type of actions or assertions, you just don't want to be a part of anything to do with your organization, then the disengagement has sunk to its lowest level, and action must be taken at this point. You've got to break the cycle.

Time to Take Responsibility

You've assessed your attitude. You know where you are. You've got the self-awareness to determine what type of contributor you are (if you're the negative one. Or, do you have enough objective enthusiasm remaining from being hired that you can see that it's truly the environment?). Now you must decide what you want to do about it. How do you affect, modify, change, improve, alter, or eliminate that behavior to overall contribute to the organizational environment that you're currently a part of?

You *must* diagnose the problem in such a way that you determine a defining answer to these questions: Is this a simple extraction of one element or another, or is this a more severe situation that must be treated systemically? It's a lot like anything else that's difficult in your life in that you've got to be willing to take a hard look at your own life and the way you're behaving and say, "Yes, I have a problem. Here's it is, and this is what I'm going to do about it."

Negativity's Influence on Employee Retention

Negativity can also take its toll in terms of employee retention. Even if an employee walks through the doors with the initial high level of enthusiasm, as soon as he is repeatedly exposed to the "negativity experience", then he is faced with two options: He can become part of the cycle (because in your organizational culture that's the norm), or he hopes that he can sustain his level of enthusiasm enough to break it and walk away. If this person falls into the cycle, that's one more individual on an organization's payroll taking money to be less creative, less innovative, a waster of time, and further promote lower morale. Employee turnover is expensive enough as it is without the second and third order effects of further decreasing the remaining employee morale and spreading a negative reputation in their next workplace.

When an organizational culture is rooted in negativity, there's one thing that's going to deteriorate faster than anything else: loyalty of those who truly believe in the company's mission. The loyalty that's lost is irreplaceable, and it's only going to be redeveloped with an entire cultural overhaul that comes with a change in practice or personnel. Maybe, you're the departure that needs to happen. Maybe that the relationship in the organization is so far gone that it's not salvageable in terms of your ability to contribute.

So... What now?

If you're fortunate enough to live and work in an organizational culture that has established a mentorship program, and you've got someone whom you trust in the workplace to go to, this is a critical time to bring that individual into the conversation. If you decide to develop a plan for improving your behavior and counteract negativity, then they'll be the ones willing to hold you accountable and keep you on track. They'll be the ideal people to help you talk about some sensitive issues and concerns that normally aren't so easy to talk about, and maybe you don't want to bring home to your spouse or into your personal life. If there's a resource within the workplace to consult, use it. Make a commitment to confining the negativity within the workplace as much as you can. Through focusing on problems with the workplace, while exclusively in the workplace, you'll experience a higher level of positivity in your personal life by not allowing the organizational negativity to seep into areas is doesn't belong.

If you've admitted you have a problem and are committed to attempting its resolution, then now is the time to start thinking about what you want that plan to look like. What type of accountability would be best served by your accountability partner or by your mentor whom you've already had the conversation with? Set goals for what you want to change. Think about your workplace 30, 60, 90 days from now, and decide what you're going to do today that's going to make things different tomorrow when it comes to behaviors. Consider giving yourself a five-minute incubation period whenever you receive an e-mail that's potentially upsetting (remember how much time I would have saved myself, my coworker, and my supervisor if I'd only waited just a few more minutes and allowed the information to sink in).

Make a list of negative behaviors and the touch points for improvement that you can see over the course of the next week. Discuss those with your mentor and decide to implement certain changes and goals concerning how your employment relationship with your organization is going to change over the next 90 days.

While it may be difficult (as most truly introspective exercises are), looking in depth at your own workplace behaviors and where you've evolved in terms of your contributions may help you eliminate the possibility that you're contributing to your own discontent more than you previously thought. The initial admittance that you've become more of a workplace divider as opposed to a cultural unifier will serve no real benefit unless followed up with a specific and measurable plan of action to move forward or a time line to move on to different opportunities. Consider the concepts presented here as an opportunity to evaluate your place in your current culture, and if there's a gap between where you are and where you want to be, then utilize your recently-achieved self-awareness to chart a course to healthier behavior and productivity. Look forward to being able to answer honestly the question "Is it me?". If after your reflection you determine that your environment and your role within it are beyond repair, then once again, congratulations on your decision to quit!

Chapter 3
Start Producing, Quit Complaining!

Take Home Message:

- At times, we feel like we know who and what we're supposed to be but just don't have the right tools; thereby, how we respond to this realization determines our organizational success

- Sometimes things just suck, and everyone has the ability and the right to complain

- Complaining without action is a waste of time and a killer to productivity, but if assessed for a root cause and coupled with a targeted approach it can be healthy

- An optimistic point of view can be as contagious as complaining. Healthy organizations not only get this but also prove it through strong mentorship and onboarding programs

---

Christopher Moltisanti: You ever feel like nothin' good was ever gonna happen to you?

Paulie 'Walnuts' Gualtieri: Yeah. And nothin' did. So what? I'm alive, I'm survivin'.

Christopher Moltisanti: That's it. I don't wanna just survive. It says in these movie writing books that every character has an arc. Understand?

Paulie 'Walnuts' Gualtieri: [shakes head]

Christopher Moltisanti: Like everybody starts out somewhere, and they do something, something gets done to them and it changes their life. That's called an arc. Where's my arc?

HBO's *The Sopranos* is going to go down as the greatest show of all time in many people's list of the top cable TV shows (at least in mine it will). That's the first time that America could rally behind a bad guy, in James Gandolfini's Anthony Soprano JR. My favorite character from the entire series was not Tony, or Meadow, or Silvio Dante (who was played wonderfully by Bruce Springsteen's front-man, Steven Van Zandt) but Michael Imperioli's Christopher Moltisanti. Christopher was my favorite because I saw him as the most consistent throughout all episodes. Christopher was one of those guys who, no matter how "bad" he was, no matter how impatient and ill-tempered, and how many poor decisions he continued to make, I always found myself pulling for Christopher a little bit. A lot like Jesse Pinkman from 'Breaking Bad' if that's a little bit more your speed.

Christopher starts out as a glorified errand boy in the earlier seasons. The first time you meet him, he's trying to negotiate with a consultant over a waste management dispute (chasing him down in his new Lexus), as he's Tony's driver. As the show progresses, he makes his way up the chain, eventually becoming a captain of the Soprano crew with his own group and his house in Jersey and a family of his own. Tony always refers to Christopher as his nephew even though they aren't blood related, as Christopher was on his wife Carmela's side; but it's apparent from the very first time that you meet him that Christopher's has a desire to better himself, which drives his aspirations towards doing more and inching more under Tony's wing. Tony definitely shows a soft spot for that from beginning to end.

Christopher is the type of character who never quite puts it all together at the right time. He's on and off drugs from beginning to end, he's never in a fully sober state of mind for one complete season, and he continues to make mistakes that you think are going to cost him at any point. Christopher tries to show some initiative early on in the first episode by killing a rival associate. He goes out with one of Tony's initial captains and tries to make a reference to *The Godfather*, which he misquotes completely ("*Louis Brazzi sleeps with the fishes*"). Now, you think this is something relatively simple, but this historical misstep provides a little bit of an insight into who Christopher Moltisanti actually is as a character. Through the entire series, the viewer gets the impression that he was trying to be something that he wasn't, and that's indicated by his misquoting something that the viewer would assume every gangster would know. He knows what he wants to say- but doesn't actually have the tools to say it.

Chris mentions from time to time that he feels he doesn't quite fit into the organization. One time in particular is when he is shot and thinks that that is his ticket to being "made." As he'd sacrificed, obviously, for the organization and the family and had anticipated that actually giving his blood was the ride to the top, he now believes himself to be an official part of the Soprano family he'd been looking for. When it doesn't happen, he continues to spiral into a mindset of anger and disrespect as his mindset transitioned as a result of realizing the toxicity of his environment.

FYI

Toxic-Shock Transition: *The moment that employees realize that their organization isn't the environment they initially perceived, and their view of the organization shifts from one of enthusiasm into one that could lead to detriment and disengagement.*

One quality that's consistent about Christopher (along with the drug use) is a constant complaining and increasingly less subtle levels of discontent. Christopher, for all intents and purposes, was the embodiment of the disgruntled employee. Those of you who have seen the show know what happened to Christopher towards the end of the series. Tony and Christopher are in a car crash, and Christopher tells Tony that he's never going to pass a drug test, even though Tony tells him previously that an "aspirin had better be the last drug that [he] ever takes". Out of some twisted view of love and compassion, Tony ultimately has to cut his losses and eliminate the liability that is Christopher Moltisanti.

So what's the point here? Many of us are the Christopher Moltisanti of our workplaces – I've even been there myself. We really want to fit in, we really want to do the right things, we want to impress those whom we feel are making an investment in us, but at the end of the day when we try to dig down deep for the tools, we just find that we don't have a big enough shovel. That analogy may be a little dramatic, but if we don't make the moves to correct the course within our current organization and either adjust behavior or remove ourselves from that "family", ultimately the organization will reach a point that it must make a decision and cut your liability on its own.

Right now, as you're reading *Just Quit Already!*, you're in control. Right now, you hold the power to decide what the next step is in your organizational journey and your employment relationship with your current company. Choose not to be the Christopher. Decide to look introspectively at the behaviors, analyze them, and make the decision to adjust your course or chart a new one.

The Ripple Effect of Complaining

Earlier, we referenced Christopher's primary behavioral trait as someone who was always complaining about something. Let's talk about that for a minute: complaining in the workplace. Bottom line: everyone, whether you're male or female, and regardless the stage in your individual careers and profession that you are, you have the right to complain. Why? Because there's numerous situations that are worthy of expressing discontent! There's a lot of situations, circumstances, and policies that simply "suck", for lack of a better term. There are a lot of things that are going to make you unhappy, and you need to vent every once in a while. I had a boss who graduated as an engineer from MIT before attending business school, and one bit of advice that he shared with me that I'll always remember is "Think about the physics of complaining," he said "and always vent up." What a very MIT way of explaining how to express discontent.

There's a solid amount of wisdom in that certain scenario, because you may be sitting in a break room or at the lunch table with your coworkers, and it may be the natural thing to share a bad situation or experience where you feel that you're justified in complaining (and you may be), but think about the overall effect on the culture that comes from having that conversation laterally and especially when you have that conversation downward with your subordinates. All of the sudden, your coworkers are looking to their left and right to you, and your subordinates are looking up to you as someone who possesses an underlying state of discontent with the organization, whether that was your intent or not. So, when it comes to complaining, consider the potential effects of the initial action, and always complain (vent) up (towards your manager or supervisor). Or, just take your complaints outside of the organization altogether, while being respectful of your personal life. So, while it is your right to complain, and it is understandable that you're going to do it from time to time as the need arises, it should also be done with caution and certainly in the most appropriate environment.

Complaining contributes to the toxic workspace referenced earlier, and once again, in the spirit of the "maybe-it's-me" mentality, I want you to think about the way that you express yourself, not just with behaviors and actions, but specifically with regard to complaining.

Think back to your different working environments and consider a hypothetical employee. We have all worked with an employee at one time or another who it becomes very easy to complain about. When I think back to my first high school job at a veterinary clinic, we had one employee who joined our team from another facility who simply worked "differently" than the existing team members.

What partially defined our team was the common need to converse and complain about the wrongs done in the workplace. Regardless of what stage in life that we were in (some employees were older and some were younger), we found ourselves bound by our discussions and complaints about a new employee. We whined about his overall demeanor and the way that this person approached clients, the way that he arranged certain medications in the cabinet, the way that he spoke with the doctors. Once again, we never vented upwards (in the sense that we never shared our concerns or complaints with the bosses because nothing was unethical, or immoral, or illegal) because it was clear that this person was just different, and complaining in that one particular sense seemingly unified our existing team. From the insider's perspective, all the complaining was a positive thing because we had one more commonality to talk about. But as an outsider, we'd limited our team's potential by excluding one and thereby cemented a culture that was exclusive by design.

Consider this: If you were the new employee whom coworkers were complaining about, you would find it more difficult to maintain your enthusiasm through resistance and toward contributions and results. Complaining in the workplace gives outsiders the appearance that things may be worse than they really are, especially when they're new to the organization. When the employee has his first sit down in the break, room and all he hears are complaints about fellow employees (possibly the person who was their hiring manager, maybe someone that referred them to the organization) or the organization, his first touch point is nothing but negativity which contributes to a toxic-shock transition. At that point, the message has just been delivered that complaining is just a normal part of doing business. Perhaps, you've just sent the message that maybe it's an expectation, and if you want to fit into this group and be part of this crowd, then you must bring something negative to the table. Once again, it may not be the intent, but it certainly is an unintended consequence of sharing negative opinions for the sake of finding unity. This is an area where organizations with strong mentorship cultures can usurp the seasoned complainers who are sharing their opinion and establishing a common bond with others.

We previously spoke about escalation in terms of the way that one situation or example can lead to another and thus potentially spiral out of control. When you're complaining and talking laterally to your coworkers (as-in, you're not necessarily venting up to seniors), you can get into this conversation of one-upmanship. I remember once in the Marine Corps (the Marines do have a saying, "If they're not complaining, it's not training!" in order to remind everyone that it's supposed to be hard), I worked for an individual who was notorious about coming in at the very last minute and asking for a project to be done. I remember I had already collected my stuff at the end of the day. I'd packed up and was ready to depart, and I'd walked down the catwalk to my good friend's office. I stopped to check out for the day. As I was saying goodnight, my boss came around the corner, and he said, "Agh! I can see that you're already packed up, but I've just found out that we've got a brief to do for the new CO (commanding officer) tomorrow morning. I'd like to go ahead and get that done, if you don't mind?" Well of course, I minded, but I also understand the supervisory relationship that I was in. So, I turned around, went back to my office, unpacked my computer, set it back up, logged back in, and began to work on the *PowerPoint* presentation, which added approximately another 90 minutes.

So the very next day, I stopped to see a colleague, and the first comment out of my mouth was "can you believe that guy? I was almost out the door, and he has the audacity to come and call me back in to build a brief that he's supposed to be giving. He had to intentionally get up from his desk and walk five minutes to come find me. He could've had three slides done by then!" The immediate response out of my friend's mouth was not, "Yeah, I can't believe that", or "That's part of it", or any level of understanding, but it was another complaint that was targeted to be worse than mine. His complaint was about his boss who had asked him to redo a fitness report (a military performance evaluation) that he'd authored on another Marine that was then due at twelve o'clock the next day. Well, not to be outdone, I said "Yeah, well not only did he ask me to prepare the brief, but this morning I had to deliver the brief on his behalf because he had to fly to Australia to surf...and I took him to the airport!"

When you get into this back and forth kind of conversation about how bad things are, you lose focus on the positive things that are going on in the organization. All the time that we spent complaining about relatively insignificant things would have been better spent focusing on the larger objectives and strategic imperatives of the unit. We killed about 15 minutes of brainpower while focusing on something negative! Yet, while everyone has the right to complain, it's important to note that we certainly don't get paid to do so.

In addition to wasting time and productivity, complaining can often fill employees with a profound sense of hopelessness. The more you complain, the higher the degree of expectation that your circumstances are going to get so much worse. If employees begin to perceive that the organization is in a downward spiral, then it will immediately kill not only the productivity but the creativity and innovation. Complaints immediately suck all creativity from that workplace like an Oreck XL.

The Cycle, Revisited

Again, negative conversation leads to negative thoughts, followed by negative action and destructive behaviors. It's no wonder that you're unhappy if you're in a place that is favoring that sort of complaint-driven atmosphere. I recall at one organization there was an effort by Human Resources to curb the conversational complaining by the employees and confine them to a suggestion box (aka the "Black box"). The concept worked to some degree, as the complaints were sent out by e-mail to all of the employees with a management response to each of them on a monthly or semi-monthly basis. This became problematic as we witnessed the transcendence of the concept of anonymous complaining turn into a collection site for intolerance and bigotry as employees took the veil of anonymity to interject opinions which were not designed to be productive, just distracting. This was able to be reversed as an innovative Human Resources manager transformed the "black box" into the "values box" and created an outlet for employees to recognize one another (and even management) for performing an act or making a contribution that was in line with the company's values.

In the cycle of negativity, people who are currently experiencing negative thoughts, feelings, and behaviors are going to thrive in a complaint-driven environment but not in a constructive way. Because complaining, as part of a culture in itself, favors negativity, it will breed negativity. Complaining is almost contagious in the sense that it does expand a culture where people feel they need to contribute something negative just to be relevant, which has proven that the only thing that comes out of those are not close, personal productive relationships but shallow, counter-productive, and oftentimes detrimental relationships.

If your workplace conversation is solely built on complaints, then how much time do you leave yourself for productive and positive things and ideas that get you excited about working in the organization in general? Getting back to my previous example with my colleague, if we had only gotten together to talk about the things that were negative within our work environment - our horrible bosses and the toxic culture - we probably wouldn't have a very virtuous relationship. Fortunately, as we were stationed in an area that was conducive to spending a great deal of time in and out of the office (Hawaii, FYI), we found plenty of topics to talk about: the beach and the islands, and the exercises we were doing, our waning golf game, and our upcoming travels with and without the military. Our relationship was subsequently founded on common interest that were more important than our complaints about the current work environment because we forcibly made it a priority to establish a relationship not founded on the negativity that we sometimes found as common ground.

Optimism, Pessimism, and the Employee Experience

How do the effects of complaining effect the productivity of newly hired team members? Oftentimes, new employees don't have the luxury of bonding with their newly met coworkers prior to their first day on the job. Because they walk through the door into a culture of complaint, they feel that that's the only way that they can find their home from the very beginning. Hence, the need for a strong onboarding and orientation process. When organizations make a commitment to growing their employees from a platform of values and inclusiveness from pre-hire to retire, they'll find that they're not only furthering engagement from the beginning but they're also curbing the desire for complaints upfront as employees first recollection of the organization is an investment in them. This isn't inherent with all great companies but is an added bonus to a very targeted and strategic approach to employee engagement. Studies show that a higher-energy onboarding process laced with positivity will lead to a more optimistic employee in the first thirty-days.

Psychologist Martin Seligman actually researched pessimism versus optimism in terms of life expectancy. Seligman deduced that people who view the world in a positive light experience a great degree of success that goes beyond just the workplace. One, their overall enjoyment of life is higher. They also have more friends in terms of quantity and quality. Their social life is existent outside of the workplace break room or the smoke pit. They tend to be healthier by multiple medical measures. They live longer, and by more metric than one, they find a greater degree of success at work. Now, success can be in terms of monetary success, promotion rate success, appreciation and advancement opportunities, and overall productive relationships.

Pessimists and complainers, however, may often make the most noise, and perhaps they get the most attention (some of you may have heard the phrase that the "squeaky wheel gets the grease"). However, in this case, the grease may be distributed, but it may be breaking the company. Whereas the optimist, who speaks and offers insight very strategically and appropriately, will oftentimes find a greater work-life satisfaction, workplace engagement, and overall positive employee experience. Complaining drains the happiness, motivation, creativity, and ultimately the fun from an entire organization. Seligman also asserts that the pessimist's viewpoint is one that takes his shortcomings as a personal failure as opposed to a professional limitation. It's clear that this toxicity can dangerously seep into the personal life if not identified and addressed.

I remember one episode of *The Office*, (which is in my humble opinion one of the best TV shows for learning the do's and, especially, the don'ts, of human resources) where character Dwight Schrute mentions that all of the good information and gossip about the company goes on at the water cooler, which he said was a detriment to him as he brings his own water to work. However, in the next scene, you see that he has moved the water cooler next to his desk so that he can become a part of the 'scuttlebutt', as he calls it. Now, I'm not saying move the water cooler so you can have more access to the complaints that occur in the workplace, but I'm saying that if you're truly committed to assisting and furthering the organization, then put yourself in a position to have that influence. Whether it be saying a little here and there with a positive twist or not saying anything at all in situations where you previously may have had a negative contribution, the result is that there is a spirit of complaining to fit in and complaining to contribute.

FYI

Scuttlebutt: *a nautical term used to describe the cask used to serve water; evolved as a slang reference to gossip or rumors.*

Your role in your current organization may affect your ability to influence the level at which complaining is occurring; after all, you may be "only one" individual; however, you're one individual who's facing a very critical time where you must decide whether or not you're a part of the problem or part of the solution. If you're at a point in your career with this current organization that you can actively remain as part of the solution and continue to contribute something positively without embracing a decaying self-confidence and personal life, then the best contribution for you in this particular aspect may not be to play the role of the moral police and correct everyone who has a complaint but to intentionally try to control the flow and the feel of conversations at the touch points where complaints usually occur.

The Positive Effects of Role Models

One interesting finding about behaviors at the workplace is that new employees have been found to mimic the behaviors of those they associate with most. For instance, when it comes to complaining, the more you hear it, the more you'll do it; however, within organizations with strong mentorship programs, there is an intentional effort to demonstrate positive behavioral traits to new hires. What you see demonstrated, you will likely do, and what you repeatedly do, you're likely to believe.

For example, I was fortunate to have the CFO as a phenomenal mentor when I worked at a family business. He had been there for more than a decade and was clearly one of the organization's most trusted advisors and confidants. I found that through our conversations and my questions, I began to interject some of his leadership style and approach into my own way of performing my work because I recognized, even if only subconsciously, that how he operated obviously worked! My mentor was an expert accountant, a subject that I studied because it was a graduation requirement and then never really intended to use again. Because it was apparent that accounting was a discipline that was important to him, I often made a point to ask him about it. Through the course of our relationship, I not only saw an in-depth view into what it took to be successful in the organization culturally, but I also gained a new professional perspective in terms of evaluating the success of a business from an industry-leading CPA. The mentorship relationship, whether formal or informal, will pay dividends in terms of employee engagement to those organizations that choose to utilize it.

The Millennial (Generation Y) Interpretation

Let's be honest, the Millennial generation has been labeled at times as the absolute worst (and they know it). The reason that this can be attributed to their constant promoting of negative thoughts and feelings is because they have had their entire professional careers as a platform to do so. It's very likely, when you grow up as part of the Facebook generation in the digital age, that your emotional intelligence is oftentimes rooted in "liking" and "sharing". The immediate response, when posting something in terms of a status update, is that the emotional feedback and rate of success will be determined by which post generates more interest over another. If we place in our status as having a bad day or that our significant other broke up with us, or our dog is at the veterinary hospital, we monitor which posts create an immediate surge of responses, support, and affirmation that makes us feel good. All of a sudden the epinephrine and the hormones rush out of control as we like the attention of being consoled, affirmed, and noticed. All we did was share a little bit about something that made us unhappy. We experience similar feelings when we express things that make us happy in our lives, and thus see that people still support us. But, it's easy to see that people are more publicly compassionate when we share with them information that depicts what is going wrong, and we reach out through our always-reliable social media in search of that affirmation.

This generation, more than others, is conditioned to the idea of sharing information and getting an immediate return or immediate feedback. So naturally, there is an assumption that this mentality is transferrable to the other network of people with whom they are in constant contact, as in the workplace. In terms of negative employee behaviors, the workplace isn't necessarily designed as the same platform as a social media following. One, because not everybody that we work with wants to follow us or values our opinions in the same way. Secondly, it's multi-generational in terms of the way that people perceive certain forms of input and types of information that is shared. Unlike social media, the workplace network isn't customizable based on the selection of membership by the employee. Lastly, the Millennial generation must understand that every opportunity where more than one person gathered is not an opportunity for social commentary (not everyone speaks in terms of Facebook statuses). Because of our constant connectivity to our social media platforms, it's quite easy to see why we believe that, but in many workplaces across the continent of the United States and beyond, that is not the case. This is why the millennial is constantly attached to his phone, constantly seeking support for his complaints and hardships and constantly sharing how he feels via his "News Feed."

Your Formal Forum for Complaining

Action and change will only come as a result of complaints if the complaining is targeted at a company's strategic plan that in turn incrementally pursues a specific end result and utilizes the right forum. Perhaps, an employee opinion survey that's conducted on a quarterly, semi-annually, or annual basis is the only time you have to truly express your opinion on the direction of the organization. Maybe that's the only time the organization allows that you get a little bit more assertive with the things that you're unhappy about in this controlled environment. Regardless of the formal or informal forum created, the employee wishing to take action must determine the underlying root causes of the complaint and then decide if he is within the scope of repair, or if he is just another behavioral by-product of the negativity cycle which some employees have found themselves in. In any case, mere complaining without advocacy is going to lead to disruption of the workplace, and advocacy without facts and strategy will fall on deaf ears.

Self-Assessment: What' About Me?

So once again, as you're asking yourself the question, "Am I the problem?", examine very closely not only the behaviors you exhibit but also the conversations that you have and the complaints that you make in your current organizational culture. Are you considered a divider or a unifier within your company's culture? If you're an employee who still has the desire to contribute, it's okay to admit that from time to time things just stink, and then you'll have the desire and right to complain. The situational awareness of understanding your environment and the current negative forces in place, coupled with the ability to channel your complaints toward targeted results, will transform your complaints from white noise of negativity to realistic results of forward progress. Complaining aimlessly without action is a waste of time, so commit to stop wasting and start working! If, however, the complaining is rooted in a much deeper cultural toxicity, then keep moving forward towards the exit sign - as you're making the right decision!

Chapter Four
Everyone's a Winner! (Except when they're not)

> *Take Home Message:*
>
> • The contemporary workplace is a reminder that not everyone can win all of the time
>
> • Competition and falling short of success builds resiliency and strengthens character, contributing to a more valuable employee long-term
>
> • Promotions aren't handed out. Sometimes, we should "Stop Asking, Start Producing!"
>
> • When it's the right time to discuss moving forward in an organization, ensure that you know the Who, What, When, Where, Why, and How of your request. Emotion without data is only half the battle

Picture a successful-looking CEO-type standing and looking out the window of a Manhattan high rise, speaking a confident monologue regarding his success when an employee enters while looking intently at her phone and texting incessantly....

CEO: "It took twenty-five years of work and sacrifice to claw my way to the top of this company, but finally, I'm here. "

Employee: "Boss, I know you're talking to yourself by the window, but I need a promotion."

CEO: "I'm sorry, what do you want?"

Employee: "A promotion!"... And I don't want it, I deserve it."

CEO: "Wha...why? How long have you even worked here?"

Employee: "Three full days!"

CEO: "I'm sorry who are you again?"

This recent sketch from NBC's *Saturday Night Live* captures a conversation that managers are having all too often across the landscape of our contemporary workforce. The assumption is that if you show up, then that's enough to become promoted, recognized, or even rewarded. That stems from some things that we've seen across multiple facets of our society, where this "Everyone's a winner" mentality has certainly started to take hold.

I remember even in my own life thinking back all the way to 1995, I was participating in our schools "Field Day". Since everyone had to participate in something, I was selected to run the 50-meter dash. Truthfully, I was not a runner. I wasn't a sprinter. I didn't even care for team sports, as something about the concept of playing as hard as you could and still losing at no fault of your own never really sat well with me. So, when it came time for the relay, there were six of us competing, and I ran as hard as I possibly could for having worn blue jeans (can you see how concerned I was for my performance?). I came in fifth out of six, so by no known standard was I even competitive. I didn't just have bad day; I just wasn't good. However, when I crossed the finish line, I was ushered over to an area where there wasn't just a platform for first, second, and third places. There was a stage - a platform for all six of us! A place for everyone to stand on, a grandstand for everyone to get his picture taken, and a podium by which we could hear our name called for a seemingly life-changing performance. I even got a ribbon that I could take home with me. It wasn't the normal primary colors of winning: blue or red or white. I'm pretty sure it was magenta or something like that. Bottom line: in no way, shape, or form should I have been recognized for that pitiful performance, but hey! I showed up, and I guess that was worth something.

This type of mentality where if you show up, you're rewarded, can detract from the individual's actual ability to evaluate not only their self-worth but also their professional worth when it comes to their contributions to the workplace or an organization. When it starts at an early age, and those of you who are reading this and have children will understand, it will prove to be more difficult to acclimate to a competitive work environment where from time to time you may actually lose. The "Everyone's a winner" mentality is not actually helping when it detracts from building realistic self-esteem and self-awareness.

This artificial reinforcement of excellence and performance creates the illusion that everyone should be rewarded, not for anything substantial he contributed but just because he's made the decision to show up. When you expand that, and you're constantly reminding others how much they're appreciated for simply participating, when you promote the idea that everyone on the team deserves a trophy, then it waters down and devalues the concept of having a competitive edge: the concept of winning. The competitive edge is one of the few true separators of potential employees. Most will enter the workforce with certain skills required to do the job, but the organization will provide an opportunity to prove who wants success the most. The point is that *if* you're not understanding what it's like to put in effort and pursue success at a very early age, then how can you truly understand what it's like to put in an effort and propel yourself and your career in the workplace?

Pittsburgh Steelers' defensive player, James Harrison, came under some of scrutiny from multiple media outlets because he had his two sons to return participation trophies that they had received. He backed that up and said that he "believed that everything in life should be earned,", and that sometimes, "you have to realize that your best is not enough, and that should drive you to want to do better" not just simply getting rewarded for participating and not just simply getting rewarded for showing up. Participation is what you do when you fail to compete, and no organization is going to put someone on their payroll who simply participated in its hiring process.

That's exactly what's happening with conversations like the *SNL* sketch above. Employees show up, which is deemed good enough; consequently, good enough can lead to promotion and advancement, bonuses, incentives, et cetera. Once again, in the maybe-I'm-the-problem mentality, let's think of the phrase, "Stop asking. Start producing" when it comes to pursuing success and happiness in the current workplace or in the workplace of the future.

From a human resource's perspective, this is an excellent mentality to have for a prospective employee because within that self-awareness concept and understanding that showing up is not enough, there lies a true key to success. If only more applicants would add to their resume: "I am not looking to simply show up and do the minimum required. I will compete for my success and will not ask for a promotion until I earn it. But, if you're the company I think you are, then I won't have to ask for it." When you're not necessarily allowed the opportunity to fail and thereby given some smaller margin of error and forced to put in a little bit more effort, that's when you'll learn resilience. That's when you'll learn from your mistakes and the wide variety of emotions and experience that you have to face in a workplace, not to mention your entire adult life will certainly strengthen your character. A resilient employee is one who can handle the temporary toxicities of organizational change and push through to the next part of the business cycle with confidence.

Individuals who are proven strong of character are the most desirable employees (mind blowing, I know) because they avoid conversations like the one above that are unfounded in results and their body of work. Two, they tend to have a higher degree of focus and attention to detail and producing results because they feel that it's genuinely a reflection upon them. When it comes to asking for things before they're surely warranted, I think that it's very clear that there is one particular generation that lives this stereotype perpetually - the millennials.

The millennial generation is notorious for always wanting and pursuing more, whether it's warranted or not. There is an immense amount of data that outlines the millennials' frequency of moving from job to job; asking for promotions, pay increases, or title changes even if it comes with no real upward movement within a certain hierarchy because of the way that it makes them feel. It reminds me of a Chris Rock segment from 1996. I wouldn't dare give the full context, but he talks about people who want credit for things that they're "supposed to do." That is the textbook definition example of a millennial in the workplace.

A millennial will say, "I show up on time." Well, you're supposed to show up on time, but that's not a reason for a promotion. That's a factor in retention, as it's an expectation. But, given the way that society has evolved with this instantaneous feedback and immediate affirmation of social media, why would the millennial think that doing anything other than the bare minimum in this culture of entitlement would be required to see some monetary return and advancement opportunity? It's not surprising to those who have seen it coming, but to the more conventional front-line manager, it's nothing more than an unsettling inconvenience.

One perk that employees have a tendency to ask for more than anything, and I think that most readers would agree, is an adjustment compensation. Compensation and the request for more of it oftentimes occurs frequently in the workplace because it's universally associated with "more means better". If your manager gives you more, he agrees that you're performing better, and the relationship is still accurate inversely. If an employee isn't having the conversation with his boss, odds are that he's having it with co-workers or friends or his spouse outside of the office: the conversation of what life would be like if he simply earned more money.

How to Ask for a Raise, and Get It!

If you are discontented with the amount of money you earn, there are guidelines to follow to ask for more compensation that will give you a better chance of getting a raise. Instead of moving into your supervisor's office and possibly being unprepared for the conversation, there are tools available to you to help mentally prepare for pursuing confidently what you want to achieve.

The idea behind crucial conversation preparation is a very simple philosophy: Who, When, What, Where, Why, and How. Also known as the five Ws and an H, something that comes from military operations planning as you define your mission. This is the way that you move through a series of directions when you're giving an order and its subsequent instructions. As you would imagine, there is very little margin for error in military operations finding, and it's amazing how these six simple questions, the five Ws and the H, can lead you from blank space to a relatively sound mission development. The compensation conversation is certainly no different, as your mission is to clearly, concisely, and accurately get your point across.

Who

The first thing that you want to define is "who?". Who are the people whom you're going to be addressing? Do you work for a board of directors? What are the professional backgrounds of the individuals who are involved? Understanding where people came from in their own professional career and drawing a parallel at least acknowledging their own professional trajectories will help better manage your expectations for how your request will be perceived. Depending on who and how many players are at the table should shape the type of presentation that you prepare. Hopefully, you've worked in your current organization long enough that you can understand what's important to your boss in terms of measurements of success and results. The other question to consider is the organization's history with your peers, colleagues, co-workers, and other individuals throughout the company. Are you asking to change the organization's 75-year history, or is what you're requesting reasonable compensation based on the precedent set by management and the current financial state of the organization? Come to think of it, has anyone gotten a raise recently? Is it that you haven't been given one in what seems to be a significant amount of time, or has there just not been any across the board?

When considering the personnel that are going to be involved in the compensation decision, if it's anything other than one manager with a stroke of a pen, then it will prove beneficial to think one or two levels above your boss when structuring your justification. As your manager will probably be thinking through how to justify your request to more senior leadership, the easier it will be for you to outline your own justification. This technique is going to increase your preparation time but may just pay off in the end – in every sense of the word.

It's important to have a full 360-degree understanding of the people involved before moving further into your conversation preparation. You don't ever want to say to your boss that you don't feel that you're being paid "fairly" without having some substantial, concrete results to back up that claim. When you're phrasing the conversation, you may want to consider asking for a specific pay increase or plan for continued financial growth.

Also, anticipate having to site several proven examples of where you've exceeded in some previous goals and metrics with a well-organized written justification. If you've exceeded your goals, then be sure that you refer to the fact that you want your compensation to reflect proportionally the exceeding of certain key metrics that are going to be easily understood by the decision makers.

One thing that Caterpillar Inc. includes in its employee reviews is whenever the conversation of salary and compensation would come up, the first thing that a manager would reference is a set of SMART (Specific, Measurable, Action-Oriented, Realistic, Time-bound) goals that were determined at the beginning of the year. Specific, measurable, action-oriented, realistic, and timely. They were set in alignment with Caterpillar's different strategic imperatives for the business unit and facility. The moment that compensation came up, SMART goal progress was the first place that the employee and the manager went together to determine if a merit-based increase was potentially justified based on how they performed in accordance with previously-set and agreed-upon terms.

When

The next "W" to be addressed is "when?". Granted, you may believe that you're at a point that you're extremely frustrated with the organization, and the only component that's going to make you stay is an increase in compensation. First of all, consider doing a more thorough review of the root cause of your discontent, as research indicates that compensation is not the only reason that people will stay with the company for a prolonged period of time. While an increase may be one element that contributes to your happiness temporarily, it will not be the only factor that solidifies your happiness within an organization. The timing of when you may have that crucial conversation and make your request is going to be equally as important as knowing who will be involved. If your company performs quarterly performance reviews or annual performance reviews at the end of a fiscal year, a calendar year, or whatever the case, then plan to have that conversation a few weeks prior to having your formal review. This way, you can reference that you know that the review is coming up on a certain time line, and your manager can anticipate that you'll want to have that discussion at that point and have some time to consider your request.

Now, if you don't have specific reviews, think about anniversaries. Every employee knows when he started, and he knows what will seem a rational interval to have enough data to have a solid conversation concerning a raise. Employees should avoid the urge to simply walk into the manager and say, "When am I going to get a raise?", or "When am I going to see a salary increase that's more in alignment with everybody else? I've been here almost a year." Perhaps, mention specifically that you know that you've have your one-year anniversary coming up, and you feel that over the course of the year, you've exceeded the goals specifically mentioned before, and you look forward to carving out some time to review performance and compensation associated with it. Be respectful of your supervisor's schedule as well, especially if it's during a financial audit or preparation for a board of directors meeting. Chances are, they'll be concerned with their own performance and the company's financial standing and would be more inclined to provide you with their full attention and consideration at a later time.

What

The next question to answer is "what?" exactly do you want? It's important to be as transparent and straightforward as possible when having that conversation with a manager because that will give you some starting point to negotiate, assuming you're not ridiculously out of scope. If you basically just say that you feel underpaid, then the manager's response is going to be based on the assumption that any increase is going to be better than where you're at. If you have a specific number based on data or based on where your position is currently paid when compared to the rest of the industry, cite examples with as much specificity as possible.

The Bureau of Labor Statistics is a great resource as well as multiple other resources that will provide salary medians for your zip code. Having that research completed, what exactly do you want in terms of a mutually agreed upon number, and what data will you reference to justify it? Where do your skills match up compared to your job description? Are you currently knocking everything out of the park in terms of job requirements? If not, do you have a specific plan of action that's going to take you from partial accomplishment to full performance? Don't be afraid to present some level of vulnerability in building that conversation to justify a very specific level of increase that you would like to see.

You might consider saying that you've "researched salaries for the zip code across the industry, and when comparing your skills and abilities with that of the job description at this organization and similar ones, you see that you're approximately $12,000 under what would be considered the fair market value for this position in this area." It's clear, concise, and immediately gives the manager a range of what you'll be asking for next. Therefore, you're "asking for a gross increase of $14,000 because of additional skill sets and perspective that your time with the organization allows you to bring to the position." Now you've indicated quite-transparently that you've done your homework; you know what you are worth according to multiple data points; and you're prepared to back that up with proven examples of exceeding performance expectations.

Where

"Where" is the best place to have a meeting where you'll be asking for something that potentially carries a great degree of uncertainty? Are you in a formal meeting setting? Are you out at a work-related social event where you can have a couple of cocktails and talk casually about all of the great things you've done? It's important to ensure that it's very clear what lines of communications exist between the two individuals having that conversation. It may be that approaching your boss outside of the office is not the best time to bring up the topic of earning a raise; that's not to say that you absolutely cannot do so.

You may also consider taking your boss on a tour of your workspace or department right before your conversation. Discuss the current state of your operations and what initiatives are coming up next, using this time as an opportunity to point out areas of improvement or exceeding metrics. Schedule the meeting, being conscious of time constraints and give him some degree of flexibility because you don't want to seem too insistent upon having that conversation on a specified time line. Doing so may make your supervisor nervous and will encourage a mentality that you're entering into that conversation prepared with an ultimatum. Have a conversation about what the boss's calendar looks like over the next couple of weeks before deciding where to meet. Find time that mutually works for you both, and begin to do your preparation.

Why

As you'll find, at the foundation of most our critical decision points lies the one-word concept that provides the most insightful justification into our actions: "why?". When it comes to increasing compensation or asking for a promotion, your level of happiness when determining how much you're able to do outside of your normal living expenses after looking at your bank account should not be a primary factor in your justification. It's likely that your management team or your board of directors is likely not going to view that as a valid concern, although emotionally it may be of critical importance to you. You've just described to them a second-order effect of "what" you want. Consider what you're doing for the organization that raises your worth above some of the tangible results they already see in terms of your expected results. If you can't detail to the organization why their current level of performance won't be maintained without your continued contributions above what is basically required, they won't understand the need for increased compensation. The key to redefining a salary range is re-educating the decision makers in terms of what is actually required to perform your job at a satisfactory level, and why your performance is, in fact, exceptional. You are the subject matter expert in what you contribute to the organization, as you are the only one with the benefit of first-hand knowledge. When this knowledge is coupled with the ability to convey the rationale for the enhancement of a compensation arrangement based on sound data points and exceptional performance, then it will be considerably stronger in your presentation. Truly understanding what your request is rooted in from a values-to-performance-based perspective will give you the much needed confidence and skill sets to holistically answer the "why?".

How

So "How?" do you capture all of these questions into one formal request that's going to appeal to all stakeholders? Remember that emotion without data will not get you what you want. Your responsibility is to present very clearly what you have done to actively "earn" the raise or promotion as opposed to why you feel you "deserve" it. Active = earning; feeling = deserving. Actively earning will predominantly win in terms of a financial justification, as it's easily translated to black and white. Oftentimes, when this level of preparation is done before an ask, you will have a much better result in terms of moving the needle from where you are to where you would like to be. Some of the preparation may lead you to realize that the time just isn't right, that you have more work to do before you can make a sound and justifiable presentation. If the data is proving difficult to find, and the performance isn't readily seen as consistently exceptional, avoid asking just for the sake of asking. Nothing will burn out a manager more than an employee who wears out his welcome when it comes to an open door of discussing promotion and advancement without a solid body of work.

When employees leave an organization, the only thing they leave behind is their body of work. When you as an employee can look within that body of work as you're growing with the organization and point to specific examples as well as demonstrate why you're an invaluable part of the family, then the compensation conversation is going to be considerably easier than when you're only rationale is that you've been there longer than the last person, and you deserve it.

Even in the most enjoyable workplaces and cultures, not everyone will win all of the time. For example, despite your best efforts, you may not just get the raise. Active and engaged employees will, or at least should, earn their promotions and raises at the appropriate time, even though some employees will continue to pursue superficial advancements incompletely and too frequently. Employees with competitive mindsets, even if they're only competing with themselves and their personal best, will build a body of work containing results of organizational progress; meaning, that for all intents and purposes, advancement will come when employees can "Stop asking and start producing" because even as personalities and personnel change,-results are undeniable.

Ask Up-Front and Avoid the Unknown

Aside from all of the questions that employees should avoid asking, there are a few that they most certainly should as they're beginning a new job, as the answers may save them from confusion or disappointment later, especially when it comes to performance and compensation. While you're in your interview and you're going through their hiring process, you want to ask the conventional questions such as scheduling, base compensation and benefits, flexible work schedules, and other factors that may come into their total rewards package to ensure that there is full disclosure about what the expectations are moving into that position.

Once you're hired and you've done the meet and greet with all of your new coworkers, find a time to visit with your manager. Maybe these are the scheduled formally as part of a mentorship relationship, but if not, schedule some time and ask some very clear questions to help set you up for success. One thing that you want to know clearly about is the way performance appraisals are done and how project feedback is given. Indicate that you'd like to discuss this at a more regular interval as you are getting started, and select a time and date to follow up. Mark the day in your calendar. Send the manager an invite via Outlook or whatever service you provide, and let him know that you're thinking about it. Have that first conversation within the first two weeks. Schedule something again within the first 90 days, and if there's nothing that's pressing between 90 and your former review, it'd be a good idea to check in again in six months. This process lets the boss know that at least you're thinking about your performance even if at times it seems that management is not.

This will allow for an upfront understanding between you and your manager for how you'll be evaluated and will hopefully give you some insight into a promotion track or compensation pathway. Different managers have different ways of doing businesses, which would be helpful to know for any new hire trying to figure out how things really work, albeit not a normal conversation in employee orientation. I recall working in one organization where on my first day my manager handed me a document titled "How to Work with Me", which was a full page of things to know; things that he appreciated, liked, disliked in the workplace; and bottom line in clear black and white what to expect. That doesn't work necessarily for everybody in terms of the way that that's communicated, but in my case, I saw it as a very transparent one stop shop for what I was getting into in terms of how this particular individual like to do business. Asking the awkward questions early in an attempt to discover how things actually operate outside of the job description will certainly give you a much better perspective on how performance will be measured and your input received.

Ensure that you understand the general scheduling in terms of availability and flexibility. Does your boss maintain normalcy with conventional time clocks? Does he check schedules every single day to know where everyone is 100% of the time? Or, is the environment a little more flexible, where as long as you're getting results, there's not necessarily a concern with where you are on a constant daily basis. Understanding how multiple levels of the hierarchy view flexible work schedules as they're becoming more and more prevalent is going to be increasingly important. This inquiry makes for a valuable conversation to have within the first day or so on the job.

A question that you shouldn't be afraid to ask within your first couple of days concerns details about the about the person who had your job before- not necessarily their personal attributes but what led to his departure and other job-relevant details. This will allow for a more educated insight into the position you've recently filled. What can you learn regarding their role in departmental successes or shortcomings? From a co-worker's perspective, it would be insightful to learn how this particular position (not the person) was perceived organizationally.

Putting it All Together

A fundamental understanding of the expectations from your organization in terms of job performance or expected results, as well as putting in the due diligence in getting to know your boss and how they prefer to discuss performance and compensation, will further set you up for success in establishing your role as a valuable part of your organization. Based on your previous work experience, your understanding of job expectations, or your interpretation of the organization's value received from your contributions, it may be undeniably clear to you that you're a winner in terms of performance. Through a comprehensive understanding of your organizational culture and your strategic approach to developing your request for additional compensation, you'll have tools to ensure that your organization agrees with you and subsequently responds accordingly. If after thorough review and discussion with management, your organization still will not ensure compensation as a reflection of your value, then it's time to keep looking for a company that will. The companies that will value you for what you bring to the table are out there, waiting for the right applicant at the right time.

Chapter Five
Know Your Role!

Take Home Message:

- It's more important to understand "why" companies, organizations, and people operate the way they do as opposed to simply what they do, and how they do it

- Lack of loyalty and trust is driving employees out of companies due to values misalignment

- "Why?" is rooted in emotion, not reason or verbiage and is a reflection of personal core values

- Core Values, when defined, will provide a platform for life's pursuits, and can be determined through assessment, performance, and reflection

- A professional strategic plan for your career is as important as one for your organization

"Would I ever leave this company? Look, I'm all about loyalty. In fact, I feel like part of what I'm being paid for here is my loyalty. But…. if there were somewhere else that valued loyalty more highly, I'm going wherever they value loyalty the most."
– *Dwight Schrute, NBC's The Office*, Season 2, Episode 5

The Office, a show that ran on NBC from 2005-2013, is viewed by many as the perfect satirical representation of the American workplace. There's the humorous boss who irritates his employees on a regular basis but deep down has a heart that is deeply rooted in the people who show up every day to make the company run. There's the conniving number two man who is consistently trying to maneuver his way into the top seat; an evolving love interest; a mediocre temp who believes he's destined for more than the current position; and the Human Resources guy who everyone (especially the manager) despises. One of the most entertaining characters outside of the genius delivery of Regional Manager Michael Scott by Steve Carrell, is Rainn Wilson's Dwight Schrute, the loyal Assistant (to the) Regional Manager. While Dwight's contribution to the show is entertaining from season to season, the above quote proves to be a bit more insightful than we may initially find as comedic, as Dwight's reference to his values and the workplaces role in being aligned with them resembles the sentiments of today's employees when it comes to what they need in an organization. Everyone knows "what" they want, yet very few can truly explain "why".

For anyone who has asked my opinion of the role of "values" in leadership and organizational development over the last several years, I have very easily rated loyalty as one of my top core values that I look for in an effective employee. Case in point- the things that I fell in love with early on in my development from childhood into adulthood, to this day I am still very much committed to. For instance, if we think about 1999, Monday night, eight o'clock, you'd find me sitting in the living room in front of the TV watching the USA network waiting for the beginning of *Monday Night RAW*. The reason was not necessarily for the action or the actual wrestling or anything about the elaborate production…but there was The Rock. When I saw The Rock come on stage and take the microphone, I saw an individual command thousands of people with a few sentences of carefully chosen words. From the way that he spoke, his delivery, his tempo, his charisma, the crowd's excitement, and the fans who were hanging on every word that he had to say- the energy was quite simply - electrifying. I said to myself that, "if I can speak and inspire people like that, there is nothing I won't be able to accomplish."

Fast forward a few years and I become introduced to the Texas FFA Association, which is a youth leadership organizational subset of the National FFA Organization. The Texas FFA has chapters in more than 1,000 high schools across the state of Texas, which develops young leaders who demonstrate the drive and initiative to become greater leaders and contributors in their communities. Texas FFA members are equipped with positive life skills and performance-enhancing attributes when it comes to growing and developing in their pursuit of career success. I was fortunate enough to get introduced to the leadership side of that organization and have a set of mentors whom I met throughout the course of my four-year active membership. These mentors further developed my leadership skills and showed that initiative and drive, when paired with the right skill sets, can go a long way. Until that point, everything that I had known of leadership was just theory. The Texas FFA was the platform which allowed me to experiment with some of those concepts and experience success for the first time, which developed in me a deep sense of loyalty to that organization.

A few years later while in college, a good friend of mine introduced me to the legendary Bruce Springsteen. I went to a Springsteen concert at the American Airlines Center in Dallas, Texas and watched over three hours of onstage excitement - pure adrenaline-laced rock and roll with thousands of people watching in awe as The Boss took the microphone and did what he felt he was born to do. People absorbed every lyric and every note that escaped the instruments of the E-Street band throughout that performance. As I sat in the arena in awe, I said to myself: "I have got to find what I'm that passionate about and use that passion to move people like this."

After those three examples, to this day I will still tell you that The Rock is still the greatest WWE superstar of all time; the Texas FFA is still the greatest youth leadership organization in the entire world; and Bruce Springsteen is by far the most influential artist to ever grace the stage and make music around the globe. The reason I feel this way illustrates the textbook definition of loyalty- unwavering feelings of allegiance that were established by an emotional connection that I experienced at some point in my life.

Truthfully, that is the definition of what's been missing in my working environment, and why I have moved from career position to career position. I've always entered a job and known what to do and how to do it. I have sold myself well in an interview process. I've been given opportunity after opportunity for those reasons and performed very well within the parameters of the job I obtained. If you're like me, you probably had some degree of success in what to do and how to do it, but you still feel unfulfilled. This is because what's missing in our workplace is that emotional connection; and, when there's no emotional connection, loyalty can't find an opportunity to develop. What's missing is some resonating effect, just one touch point which can serve as the catalyst for a foundation of loyalty which would sustain our commitment to an organization for years to come.

The following chapter is going to be essentially two sections. One is going to be a review of one of my favorite books when it comes to understanding your role in an organization and understanding why some people and organizations can find success and then repeat it-Simon Sinek's 2009 book *Start With Why*. You may have read the book or seen his TED Talk, and if not, it would definitely be time well invested, as the author reveals commonalities between the world's greatest leaders and companies. Reviewing that text will set us up for the second part of this chapter, which is how to apply it to our role as employees in the workplace and to understand why we are pursuing a certain job, career path, organization; moreover, it will show you what to look for in that organization to determine values alignment. If we understand the "why?" behind our decisions in the workplace, then the reasons we may need to depart from it will become clearer.

Section One: Starting with Why

Additionally, if you're deciding to depart an organization, a fundamental understanding of "why?" will be critical in determining how to examine the next opportunity with a slightly different lens to ensure that you're giving yourself the best chance to achieve an emotional connection in order to develop a sense of loyalty. Loyalty will lead to longevity in your job and career field. *Start With Why* states that "There's a big difference between repeat business and loyalty. Repeat business is when people do business with you multiple times. Loyalty is when people are willing to turn down a better product or better price to continue doing business with you." Think about that in the context of your current organization. Now, at this stage in your career you are looking to move on professionally. You're ready to go somewhere else and no longer willing to consider yourself a loyal employee in your current position. Even though you may buy the company's product or support the company's mission in one way or another, the fact remains that you're willing to depart, which is a side effect of the lack of emotional loyalty that's been developed.

In *Start With Why*, the bottom line is that there are leaders and there are those who lead. The text is about a naturally occurring pattern in the way of thinking, acting, and communicating which gives leaders the ability to inspire those who are around them: a concept that also applies to companies.

When you're in an individual contributor role, as opposed to leadership or management, the same concept applies even as you'll still possess a set of principles that can allow you to inspire those through your beliefs, your actions, and your overall achieved results that are rooted in your core values.

The first portion of *Start with Why* describes that there's two ways that we're going to see behavior influenced, and that is through either inspiration or manipulation. For those who have an open mind to new ideas and seek to create long-lasting success, they believe that lasting success requires the involvement and support of others. In order to gain the unwavering support of others, the inspiration approach must be employed as opposed to the manipulation tactic, as manipulation may create a short-term gain but not lasting results. Now, odds are if we've created an opportunity for any sort of movement in our current career, we may be familiar with the concept of manipulation because the fact of the matter is, it works.

Manipulation is about knowing what we want, how to get it, and often times who needs to be involved to make that happen. Whether that's negotiating certain price points or maneuvering our way to promotions -or even into the job itself- capitalizing on people's fears through what we may know through some facet of our relationship is the exploitation of an unhealthy connection. All are things that we can use to get what we want in the workplace but will ultimately drive cultural toxicity and short-lived success. The value of all of those techniques is that they work, but manipulation is not organizationally sustainable. Manipulation may create a short-term gain; whereas, true cultural inspiration (and the subsequent loyalty that comes with that) is a much longer-term investment in the workplace. When it comes to experiencing actual leadership, as opposed to just being led, manipulation can help you get to a certain point, maybe even to the top, but it won't keep you there forever. If you manipulate your way to the pinnacle without inspiring people along the way, then you may turn around to realize that no one is behind you because of the way that he was treated.

As employees, we all know what we want. We want to be successful in whatever we perceive that success may be. Maybe it's that we just want to make more money so we can buy the Maserati, or perhaps is we'll feel successful when we're allowed to work a flexible work schedule. There are several articles that outline the three "Fs" in the workplace that the modern employee wants: flexibility, function, and fit. That's the "what?". "Why?" the employee wants those perks resides one level of consciousness deeper.

The Overarching Organizational Mission
One of the quotes from the Sinek's text is that "Leadership is the ability to rally people not for a single event, but for years. In business, leadership means that all customers will continue to support your company even when you slip up." I was previously part of an organization that built its entire budget and yearly schedule around one large event that happened annually. Every possible marketing idea, technique, tactic, and approach was geared towards this one massive event that hosted more people than anything else that the organization conducted throughout the year. The problem is that the event was the "what" not the "why". People knew that there was an

event that they were to attend. They knew how they were going to get there. They knew who would be involved. Where the event began to become stale and lost creativity is when there was an apparent lack of clarity on "why" the event was in place. When I was beginning to make arrangements and plan for the event's theme development, I met with a dear friend of mine who is the Chief Marketing Officer for an international apparel company. She'd seen the product and was familiar with our intent, but she shared with me that the key to planning this was to "quit looking at it as a stand-alone function to attract people but as a by-product of the overarching organizational mission". Bottom line: the event needed to be nothing more than a reflection of the organization's brand and a clear presentation of its values in action. This reflection would not only engage the customer base but also remind the employees of the reason they remained committed to the organization.

One thing that Simon Sinek highlights is "the golden circle", which you'll see very clearly demonstrated on the TED Talk as it shows how leaders are able to inspire action instead of manipulating people to act. The outer layer of that golden circle is the "what". Every company in the world can tell you what it does and can even describe its product or service. Often times in interviews, the interviewer will lead with the comfortable: "Tell me a little bit about yourself", to which the employee will likely describe "what" he does. "I'm an accountant. I keep the books for company X, Y, Z and have done so for X years." It's very easy to describe the service that you provide, but that's not the insightful information to help identify cultural fit. The next layer of the gold circle is "how". Companies, for most intents and purposes, will readily discuss how they do what they do. They'll be able to tell you how they're different through a set of unique selling points designed to differentiate them from the marketplace in terms of "how" they get to the result that you're seeking. You, as an employee, may be able to readily identify that same sort of differentiation. As an employee, try to define how you interact differently with your coworkers, or how your skill sets will help bring a slightly different "what" to the organization as opposed to the status quo.

Very few companies have made a mainstream effort to share with the consumer "why" they do what they do. The answer is not so abrupt as to say, "We make this product to sell it to you to make money", as the money is one of the results. You, as an employee, know that you don't do "what" you do and "how" you do it for the sole purpose of income.

FYI: DNV-GL

Driving the necessity to understand a deeper purpose for employment, DNV-GL has the following question posted on its careers page as a message to potential applicants before applying: "Why do you get up in the morning?"

In your current job, what is the organization's purpose, and why should anyone care? Why do you feel the need to work at this organization over another? Once again, don't think about the result. Think about the larger issue in what you are seeking to have fulfilled. What is your purpose, and why should anyone care that you want to come and do business with them?

Now, most normal companies communicate from their outside in terms of their products and services, just like people. Some have a call to action: "This is what we do. This is how we do it, and this is what we're asking of you in return if you like what you hear." One company that Simon Sinek continues to reference throughout the entire text and especially during the TED Talk, is Apple. He very clearly demonstrates evidence of how Apple has differentiated itself in the marketplace by understanding what makes it different than the competition. Notably, they have the ability to provide the consumer with the reason why. If Apple were like everybody else, they would say, "We make great computers." The reality is that Apple goes a little bit further than that in terms of the way that they tell you exactly why they're in business.

Sinek draws a contrast to Dell computers in saying that Dell defined itself by what it did; it made computers. When Dell began to make an MP3 player, it flopped. People didn't feel like they could buy an MP3 player from a computer company. Apple, who defines itself by "why" they do it, was able to make an MP3 player, phones, and tablets. When Apple started with the why, the features and what it did doesn't matter as much. Sinek proposes that a marketing message from Apple may sound like "Everything we do, we believe in challenging the status quo, we believe in thinking differently. The way we challenge the status quo is by making our products beautifully designed and user friendly- we just happen to make computers." Because, he states "People don't buy what you do, they buy why you do it."

Here's how the analogies above relate to you as an employee. What you do, the services you provide, and how you get there won't matter as much as to what your goal is to attract people to believe in your why. Job selection is never really a debate about better or worse, as it's essentially a discussion about different needs. Before you spend hours on cover letters and resumes, differentiating yourself from the other applicants in terms of the "what" and the "why's" must be established first. "Why is the company in business? And, why are they needing someone in this role right now?" As well as, "Why am I the right person to be in the organization? And, what will I bring to the table?"

One thing that Simon Sinek says is that when it comes to the science of why humans are responding to the "Why" mentality, "it's not opinion. It's biology." If you look at the cross section of the human brain from top down, the levels of the golden circle correspond closely with three major levels of the brain. The neocortex corresponds to the "what". The

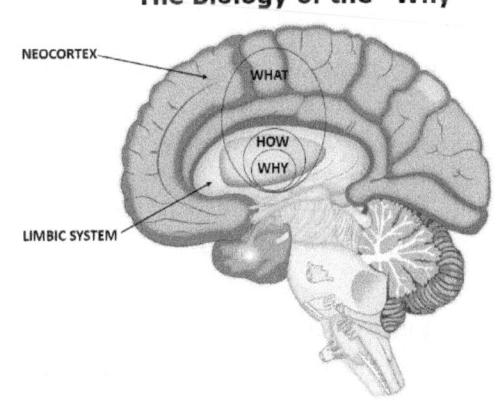

The Biology of the "Why"

neocortex is a part of the cerebral cortex concerned with sight and hearing and is where rational thought and analytical thinking originate. Now, the limbic brain corresponds to the "how" and the "why". This part of the brain is a wide-variety of structures where feelings and emotion come from and where decisions are made. This part of the brain really has no control over language, which is why it can be hard to describe your feelings at times. That's why it may be so difficult to venture beyond the just-here-to-make-money mentality and get into the hard questions of what inspires you to show up every day. Gut decisions, thinking with your heart, personal motivation…all of that happens in that limbic brain portion which controls how you feel about something and your subsequent behavior, but it has nothing to do with how you verbalize it.

Companies that fail to communicate their sense of "why" try and force decisions with only empirical evidence will take more time to develop brand loyalty. As rational thought and data are having to compete with the human emotion and personal motivation, a clear lack of organizational values will keep customers and employees uncertain of where they fit in with their sense of purpose. Imagine if the only thing Ford Motor Company advertised in its commercials was how economical the purchase of a Ford vehicle was, as opposed to pursuing the emotional response which tells the consumer why it's the right vehicle for him. When communication occurs from the "inside out" as Sinek describes, you're talking directly to the part of the brain that controls decision- making. When you as an individual can define why you do what you do and why you pursue the work environments that you have, you'll have become more prepared to communicate transparently to a hiring manager what it is that you'll need in terms of personal and professional fulfillment in a particular job.

Section Two: Working with Why

It's not just what or how you do things that delivers optimum career success, as the "what" and "how" will only create mediocrity when not aligned with the "why". When you reach a point in your career that you're experiencing that contradiction, the instability will lead to unhappiness, disengagement, and ultimate departure.

With all of this talk about starting with the "why" and "core values", the assumption is that you're an employee who is firmly rooted in a values-based life and work mentality. Or, you may be at the point of your career where you're thinking that you've never actually laid out what your core values are. Just like everything else, while determining what your core values are, you should expect that it will be a very personal, extremely introspective experience. Jim Collins made a great case for the power of core values in business in his book *Built to Last*, which I've just recently requested as assigned reading for a leadership group with whom I work. *Built to Last* is a master work of business literature that proves the benefit to a values-based organizational strategy in building a lasting business. However, if you're pursuing a new career or venture and you can find relatively easily what the company values, it's going to be hard to determine values alignment without an in-depth understanding of your own core values. In your daily life, decision-making points, and routine, your personal core values are going to guide your behavior whether consciously admitted or not; and when you get them right, you'll be able to focus your decision-making, your current career search, and your review of current job opportunity to decide with confidence if it's going to be a good fit. As with many business and leadership concepts, there's a process to help you in hacking into your limbic brain and decoding your personal values.

There are multiple ways to clarify and define individual values, but I'll share one that I prefer due to its research driven description. "Values Clarification" is an approach formulated by Louis Raths, who, along with Harmin and Simon, built upon the work of John Dewey to define seven criteria in determining core values. These criteria can be consolidated into three categories: choosing, prizing, and acting. To be truly considered a core value, the value must be chosen (category 1) freely (criteria 1) from a list of multiple alternatives (criteria 2) only after thoughtful consideration has been given to the consequences of each alternative (criteria 3). The value must be honored and internally cherished (category 2, criteria 4) and made known to other people (category 5). The value must also be translated into behaviors (category 3, criteria 6) that are consistent with the chosen value and integrated into the life style (criteria 7). It's important to note that your values will change over time in accordance with your life experiences, so knowing your values when you began your career may not have relevance today.

Defining your Core Values

The first thing you should do is find yourself some time where you know you'll be uninterrupted and then reflect. Grab a notebook and a pen and find a quiet spot to think. Begin to remind yourself of your greatest accomplishments in life so far: when you're at the top of your game; when everything was going right; when you were efficient, effective, and empowered. What were the circumstances surrounding these moments? What was driving you to succeed? How were you recognized or rewarded? Were there any central themes or objectives of the organization you were in or anything unique about the environment that made it special? If you went back in time and could provide advice to yourself, what would you say to do to ensure the same level of success and happiness?

Now, transition to the opposite end of that spectrum, when were things in your life the worst? When were you not producing at capacity, unmotivated, uninspired, and undetermined to make progress? What was it about that environment that killed your creativity? If you went back in time to this point, and could tell yourself what to avoid, how would you describe it?

Get your pen. Everything that's important to your work and life, pour it on the tablet. From one to two-word phrases to entire sentences or paragraphs, just fill up that paper. Values often stem from our purposes, goals, aspirations, internal beliefs and convictions, interests, desires, feelings, activities, anxieties, problems, and obstacles. Each of these are value indicators but are not always values. Odds are that the manifestation of one of the indicators is stemming from an underlying value which must be determined.

Articulate them clearly in writing and narrow your list to your top 20, one-word values. Let that sit for five minutes. Walk away, do something different, rest your mind before returning to it.

Now, break your list into two columns of ten and move down the list selecting one written value from each column to advance. When completed, you will have identified your top 10 "personal" values. Let that sit overnight. Come back the next day (preferably roughly the same time), make your columns, and narrow that list down to your top five core values. The reduction of the list from 20 to 10 is going to be considerably easier than 10 to 5. You may think that all 10 are important, but when you're going from 10 "personal" to 5 "core", you are determining the difference between important and critical. For example, what value can you not live or perform without?

When you have your top five, I would recommend testing their validity through the following processing questions as extracted from Raths' work on the "process of valuing."

1.) Are you proud of your values- do you deeply prize and cherish them?
2.) Can you see yourself standing up for your values honorably in public and in private?
3.) In choosing your values have you strategically considered many alternatives?
4.) Have you evaluated the strengths and weaknesses in your selected values?
5.) Have you chosen your value openly and honestly without personal or organizational pressures?
6.) Have you taken action to live or implement your values, or have a plan of action for doing so?
7.) Have you acted with consistency in living this value?
8.) Have you considered its order of importance in relation to your other values?

9.) Have you considered how it relates to the values of other personal and professional relationships, including those you interact and work with?

If you can process the values you've selected with confidence in accordance with these questions, then you're certainly on the right track.

It's also important for new teams and departments to get together to established their own core values, especially if they're going to be working together on a project that's going to keep them working together for a sustained amount of time. For instance, I was recently working with an organization and inherited a team that was meeting for the first time, so I decided to take them through this exercise so that before they started anything else, they would start with the "why".

For reference, here is their list of five considerations that their life experiences manifested in this acronym SERVE:

- **S**elflessness: showing greater concern for the organization rather than themselves during the project
- **E**mpowering Team Members: investing time to develop others to become the best version of themselves (a key tenet for most leaders)
- **R**eason: the power of the mind to think, understand and make decisions by process or values- based logic (Bottom line, if it didn't make sense, they didn't do it)
- **V**ision: establishing a clear image for a better tomorrow
- **E**xcellence: forging a first-class experience for the members which they were empowered to serve

After you've narrowed your list, spend the next two weeks finding times where they present themselves in your daily routine, personally and professionally. If the values that you've listed don't present themselves in some form or fashion throughout your work day or your time at home, odds are they're not necessarily a "core" value and may simply be an indicator. When employees are doing things in pursuit of some business results, there is always the temptation to conform to the "why" of the business. Keep in mind, that some parts of this exercise may be uncomfortable as you determine that you may possess the right values for the organization on paper but not in practice. If you aren't able to demonstrate your values freely in the workplace, it's clearly not an ideal fit.

Stepping Toward Values-based Relationships

As you're on a path towards ensuring a values-based work-life relationship, there are a few steps to consider taking to ensure you were accurate in your determination and focused in your pursuit:

First, make an intentional effort to put a list of the values somewhere that they'll be easily seen throughout your day. Starting with one on your bathroom mirror, another on your steering wheel, one as the wallpaper on your computer login screen, etc. Ensure that you don't have to look too far to be reminded of what's important.

Secondly, be prepared to talk with people about your values, especially if you're putting up reminders around the workplace: otherwise, people will naturally want to know what you're working on, and you should be confident in sharing your process and the results. This will not only strengthen your relationship with some of your colleagues, but it will also allow for greater accountability and discussion when it comes to things that are important. Unfortunately, not everyone will appreciate your efforts. Either they simply won't get it or will disagree judgmentally in what you're trying to accomplish. This isn't necessarily negative. Wherever you can afford to eliminate possible conflict by misaligned values, you should.

Third, "Assess, Perform, Reflect." Even if you're not a list maker currently, think about your day in terms of tasks you need to accomplish. Include conversations, meetings, presentations, and projects, and further consider where in each responsibility you can create an opportunity to ensure our utilization of a values-based approach. Write down next to the items in your schedule which of your core values you intend to apply. For instance, if you've determined the core value of honesty, and you're in auto sales, think about the 9:00AM customer you intend to meet with and how to ensure the most honest representation of the transaction. Go through your entire day determined to perform all tasks in accordance with your values, and then take some time to review your list at the end of the day. Consider where you could've performed differently. Reflection without action can be a waste of time, so commit to performing stronger tomorrow. You'll fall short from time to time, but so what? Embrace the fact that you're continuing to grow and develop as a person and employee because you're understanding "why."

To recap. These are the steps: write it out, talk it out, live it out. Once you've committed to your values-based approach to a job and career, you can begin to think more strategically about where your career is heading. A great mentor of mine once taught me the value of having a strategic plan: a living, breathing road map to where his organization was headed over the next five years or so. The first strategic planning exercise that I went through began the same way as every other strategic planning exercise I've done since: I define the organizational values. A personal strategic plan for your career is much the same in that it establishes a values-based road map for what you expect to deliver and receive from your employment.

Discovering and proving your top five values will allow you to create your career purpose statement (which some companies may refer to as a vision statement) in order to bring the "why" to life and begin artistically to craft your strategic plan. Successful companies have made it very clear what they believe and where they're going through their clearly defined purpose statements for all employees and consumers to use in holding them accountable. As an employee preparing to enter a new organization, you should do the same.

FYI: Mahindra USA

Mahindra USA's Rise philosophy touts the purpose statement: "We've made humanity's innate desire to Rise our driving purpose: we will challenge conventional thinking and innovatively use all our resources to drive positive change in the lives of our stakeholders and communities across the world, to enable them to Rise. Our purpose is why we exist and why we come to work every day, infusing our lives with meaning, and galvanizing us to deliver our promise."

When reviewing the example above, it's clear what the company values through their transparent delivery of their purpose statement. This degree of organizational clarity makes it very easy for an employee to determine if they'll fit in.

An employee vision statement may be as follows: "By staying true to my core values of Honesty, Integrity, Trust, and Love, I will create a culture that thrives on inclusiveness and respect in all interactions all of the time where loyalty runs deep."

If you want to take your road map more specific in terms of the position, an employee mission statement can help define the "what". For instance, "Through a values-based approach to leadership and management, I will provide a first-class Human Resources experience for all employees of CTD Worldwide." Once the Values, Purpose, and Mission are established, your career strategic plan can begin to break down into milestones of accomplishment and results on the time line you decide.

With these strategic tools at your disposal, employers and hiring managers will have a much greater insight into who's coming to the table, and what they're bringing. More importantly, having gone through this exercise and understanding at a values-level "why" you're pursuing a certain opportunity will make you a considerably more insightful applicant as you'll be able to look for similarities in the alignment of the organization.

When the Values are Skewed, the Exit is Easy

I remember leaving one job in particular where the overarching theme for my departure could be summarized with two words: *values misalignment.* Throughout the duration of my employment, it became clear that what I valued as a person and as a professional was a stark contrast to what my superior, and ultimately the organization, saw as important. As a Human Resources professional, I was part of the administrative services and support team. This means that by design, I was not in a position to make the company the same degree of profit as quickly as those in the sales or operations department. Translation: Regardless of how much effort I put into projects or initiatives, I would never be viewed as valuable as other "producers" unless the results were visible in terms of monthly cash flow. With this in mind, I worked diligently to make my position of greater importance to the boss through building efficiency into our administrative processes, strategically recruiting top producers for other areas of the business, and moving the structure of the HR department into the 21st century. Unfortunately, no increased cash flow still meant no increased value or recognition. The turning point in my professional relationship with the organization came when members of the senior management team made the decision to circumvent company policy and posted values in order to retain a "top-producer" accused of inappropriate workplace behavior. Values were important- but not as important as having a profitable month. As a principled HR professional, this event solidified my mentality that the organization was not for me. The disengagement began, and departure followed less than sixty days later. Values misalignment is a highly likely contributor to your reasoning for departing your current organization and finding an organization with the people in place who support your core values and will lead you to a more engaged employee experience and satisfied professional life. Leaving your current organization is the "what,", and if you can ensure that you've done the research to fully understand "why", then you will have taken a big step in discovering professional happiness.

Chapter Six
Quit Adding Friends, Start Making Them!

Take Home Message:
- Social media is a platform for making and maintaining connections, but it is no substitute for genuine connection between friends and coworkers

- With the rising dependency on social media for relationship management, the need for emotionally intelligent employees is greater now than ever

- Self-Awareness, Self-Management, Social- Awareness, and Social Skills are four subsets of emotional intelligence that possess specific competencies for optimal workplace effectiveness

- Evidence suggests that an emotionally intelligent culture is the key to creating an environment where employees are engaged

"But that's the funny thing about destiny: it happens whether you plan it or not. It turns out I was just too close to the puzzle to see the picture that was forming" - Ted Mosby, *How I Met Your Mother*, CBS

Every generation has a show that they'll reference for years after the show wraps, and for many, there will be no show that is referenced in one way or another more often than *How I Met Your Mother* (HIMYM). It's like *The Office* for your personal life. The show went on for nine seasons and had one of the most divisive and controversial endings for a beloved sitcom in television history. Throughout all of the shows ups and downs, it introduced America to the fact that the concept of true friendship (amidst an age of rapidly evolving social media surging parallel to the shows run) can still exist. Through all of life's mistakes, career transitions (to include quitting!), bad decisions, late nights (even after 2 AM), breakups, reunions, and tragedies, the real relationships we form are what sustains us through it all. Though life's story may be messy and at times incongruent, HIMYM proved that it doesn't have to make sense all of the time in order to remain an integral part of the same story (I mean, the yellow umbrella, c'mon. Pure genius.).

The story was tied together from the emotionally-intelligent narrative of the shows protagonist, Ted Mosby, as he shares his life's story with his children from the perspective of a much older, wiser, father figure than we were watching on the show. While there are many parallels we can draw from the way HIMYM was designed to the way that we live out our relationship stories, we don't have the luxury of the corresponding commentary from a considerably more emotionally intelligent futuristic version of ourselves to clue us in to what's actually happening. Therefore, whether it's in the living room or the board room, a conscious effort to further the development of our own emotional intelligence (EQ) will prove to be increasingly (and critically) important in your future career success. Before we can fully do that, we need to evaluate the role of one of our closest relationships, (the not so) social media. So, as you prepare to make your exit from one company and entrance into another, let's discuss the deeper levels of what type of employee you are compared to the kind you want to be.

The Social (Media) Connection

There's no question that social media has become more and more popular over the last decade and a half. I remember getting a Facebook account when it was only available for college students; now it's more of a shock when you meet someone who doesn't have one. Amidst all of the outlets for social media and digital connectivity, human beings still yearn for some type of emotional connection - some sense of belonging- in all relationships, including the workplace. There have been several studies conducted that support the idea that "true" social interaction with another human being can lead to positive mental health. Seeing as we spend the majority of our waking hours in a place other than our home, we must look at our workplace and evaluate the health of our social relationships. Research has also revealed that people with fewer social relationships tend to die earlier on average, are generally unhappier, and often times have a larger degree of disengagement when it comes to their actual connectivity to their place of business, including their coworkers, superiors, and subordinates alike.

There's no question that the internet in general has become enormously popular (and even critical in many cases) in the way that we do business. It's convenient, as it provides instant gratification when we have something that we feel that's worth sharing with the world. The workforce is currently witnessing the influx of a generation that's grown up entirely with YouTube as their primary platform for communicating information and gaining friends (aka followers that they don't really know and will probably never meet) and finding their sense of belonging. With this influx, the workplace *must* find ways to keep up with the constantly surprising behaviors of the digital generation.

Social media sites like Facebook have more than one billion users worldwide. It's an instant audience and place to gain instant attention for whatever the user feels like sharing. Users have the luxury of easily keeping in touch with people that they haven't spoken to since high school reunions or even further back than that. Social media gives us the sense that we do belong to something big, as it creates a sense that we're not really missing out on true social interactions. We have an instant scrapbook of different life events that we can review at any point in time, whenever we want to look on those memories fondly to take us to a different time and place (It's not uncommon that we do that in the workplace). There's no question that the internet and social media has offered a convenient and gratifying way to locate, reconnect, or rekindle past relationships and experiences that may have been lost without this platform.

People used to wait for letters to come in the mailbox, and in their responses they would take time to carefully draft them and ensure that the words and cursive penmanship were just right. The reality is that friendship has become in a lot of ways like cursive handwriting. When there are so many different things out there (text messages, moji's, Bitmoji's, social media, messages, Snapchats) what is the advantage to taking the time to carefully construct a physical piece of correspondence? For a solid and presentable piece of cursive writing, you can't just learn it once and immediately turn it back on as needed. It's harder to achieve a presentable skill set in the first place and even more difficult to maintain. Friendships are the same way; there's a multitude of ways to have social interaction, but the ones you want to hang on to take a bit of time and work.

When people say on social media sites that they're adding friends, what exactly does that mean in terms of a true emotional connection generally associated with the word *friend*? Is it really that instantaneous? When we say that we have 1,000 friends, what is the deeper and more emotionally significant level of that friendship? If there is a level of personal gratification from achieving that high quantity of friends in the social network, then are we using it as an excuse to step further away from those individuals whom we see on a daily basis?

We can't discount the fact that there are a lot of individuals on social media who are real-life friendships, as the social media network is also the place for preserving those connections. But, as we find ourselves as a society more dependent on instant connectivity through a smart phone or other mobile device, it's becoming more difficult to break the digital dependency in exchange for genuine relationships. As employees and individuals, there should some level of concern about a movement towards focusing predominantly on adding friends instead of truly making them, especially when it comes to the overall effect on workplace relationships. Consider some of the best friends that you would say you have, and reflect on some of the most defining moments of the relationship. Most likely, you thought of an experience together or significant time spent with one another. The relationship is built on true experiences, conversations, and some sense of growth and development you've experienced together. Your best friends have probably seen you at your worst and vice versa. Studies indicate that people put their best foot forward while interacting on social media, in a sense that the user wants people to see that things are going well for the most part.

Granted, there's a lot of opportunity to share when things are not going well because social media also provides a safety net for immediate affirmation and reassurance that things are going to be okay. But generally, people like others to assume things are great, and that they are fine, especially in a society when it's acceptable that some employees can be friends with their coworkers or even their managers or members of their board of directors, so they will try to preserve a clean and generally positive image. There are probably some instances where employees forget who all is in their network and do a status-update rant about how lousy their job is and how stupid their manager acted, which is why I highly advise determining a very specific set of people for your social network. I have committed to using Facebook for people I want to stay acquainted with for one personal reason or another (no coworkers, just friends and family only). I use LinkedIn for all of my business contacts (coworkers and colleagues) and Snapchat for my actual friends (seriously, there are only about seven people on my Snapchat list).

While our social media environments offer a great deal in terms of the instant gratification, there is no true substitute or even a supplement for the real life interactions with others and the vulnerability that is necessary to develop and maintain that relationship. As you continue to add friends and accept friend requests, don't discount the necessity to look for further opportunities in the workplace for professional and longer-lasting emotional connection. In many retirement and departure speeches, the one thing that employees say that they'll miss most is the people, not the high tech equipment or the multi-million-dollar facility, but the relationships. Online friendships will continue to be valuable, and social media presence as opposed to a mere profile will become increasingly more important as the influence of social media becomes more heavily weighted in the hiring processes of many businesses.

A popular movement currently is Tinder. Tinder doesn't require much reading; it doesn't require much input nor output in terms of your willingness to connect with another individual; all it really requires is a picture. You can make a connection (or not) with a simple swipe left or right of your finger across the screen. That type of interaction is growing the familiarity with a more superficial type of relationship, which if translated in any degree to the workplace will prove to be damaging. If the mind becomes conditioned to voting on an individual's worth based on an initial assessment, then the effort required to begin forming significant relationship will certainly be increased, as talking through the initial response will be a bit uncomfortable when you're used to quickly moving on to the next candidate.

The Emotionally-Intelligent Employee

The counter to the propagation of shallow relationships and loss of connection in the workplace is a concerted effort to develop the emotional intelligence of the employee. Many sites are commentating on the concept of emotional intelligence, which has been proven in multiple studies to be a definite driver of engagement and success. My first interaction with emotional intelligence as a concept came in my first year in the Marine Corps. Most commanders will issue to their new check-ins a command philosophy or reading list. This particular commanding officer handed me a copy of Daniel Goleman's, *Primal Leadership* and discussed the importance of having an emotionally intelligence command philosophy in terms of its effect on the workplace, troop morale, and its effect on our ability to communicate with and understand our enemy.

That was an incredibly important piece of information to deliver to a brand new lieutenant looking to fit in in a higher level of command. Although, my next commanding officer gave me season one of *The Sopranos* to further my understanding of his command philosophy (which was also extremely insightful but in a considerably different way). Both Commanding Officers were emotionally intelligent warfighters, and their commitment to grow and develop young officers was proof that they not only read Goleman's book but also lived it.

Regarding emotional intelligence, there are several authorities on this subject that I would highly encourage you to research and review their work outside of this text. The work of the experts will provide a much more comprehensive view of what emotional intelligence is and its role in the workplace. By far, my favorite author and one of the world renowned experts on this subject is Daniel Goleman. Daniel Goleman and Cary Cherniss have written, *The Emotionally Intelligent Workplace*, among many other works that they've distributed and published on the subject. The *Emotionally Intelligent Workplace* describes how to select for, measure, and improve emotional intelligence in individuals, groups, and organizations. It's an entire work dedicated to transforming what could potentially be a toxic culture into an emotionally intelligent environment where people understand each others emotional signals. From the very initial human resource hiring process to the final movement into retirement, an emotionally supportive and strong culture will create a workplace where employees can thrive in their work and enjoy healthy relationships.

In terms of a summarization of emotional intelligence as a concept, it's best described as the capacity for understanding our own feelings, the feelings of others, for motivating ourselves, and for managing our emotions effectively in our relationships. When emotional intelligence is referenced in text, it's often indicated with the abbreviation EI or EQ. When we dissect the way that we interact in a workplace as it relates to having an understanding and ability to perceive the feelings of others, we don't have to go very deep into the subject to understand quickly why it will be critical in moving forward and ahead. On occasion, emotional intelligence will be referred to as, "the people smarts." This is not generally assessed with the type of intelligence evaluation when we talk about IQ, or the intelligence quotient, which is the "book smarts". The IQ can tell provide an idea as to an individual's ability to understand and process information as opposed to his ability to interpret the way that people feel.

An understanding of the role of emotional intelligence in the workplace has a direct effect on work performance, not only yours as an individual contributor, but the individuals who work with you. An HR consulting firm researched 515 senior executives and found that the executives with strong emotional intelligence test results were more likely to propel in terms of their career success than other executives whose strengths were rooted in previous experience or traditional IQ scores. When the study references emotional intelligence test results, many of Goleman's works will include some EI examination to provide a benchmark of your current degree of emotional intelligence. A similar study involved 130 executives and demonstrated a strong correlation between how well an individual handles personal emotions and the willingness of others to work with that individual.

As you think about the behaviors of a disgruntled employee in the behavioral stage of the negativity cycle, reflect on your "gut reaction" at the prospect of having to work with him. Now, shift the lens to yourself and consider whether or not your negative behavior has affected the likelihood of individuals to volunteer to work with you. As your trajectory from an engaged employee to a disgruntled employee has continued to trend towards disengagement, the emotionally intelligent employee may have begun to intentionally distance himself. A leader/manager with positive mood interacts with individuals in a way that creates positive results. An employee with helpful attributes and strong cooperative skills, coupled with an ability to convey those skills onto others, increases his overall work group efficiency. Employees often mimic the behaviors and attributes of their leader, and an emotionally intelligent leader can create an environment for optimum engagement. When the behavior is not engaging, employees will either disrupt the process or distance themselves.

Emotional Intelligence Defined

Emotional intelligence is not based on one single characteristic but is rather a wide set of competencies that are organized into a few major subsets. The number of subsets varies from two to five, depending on which text you reference, but for our intents and purposes in discussing the workplace, we're going to focus on four subsets and 19 different competencies within them. The four subsets of emotional intelligence we'll breakdown are self-awareness, self-management, social awareness, and social skills.

Note

The following is a generic collection of information which distills findings from MOSAIC competencies for professional and administrative occupations (U.S. Office of Personnel Management); Spencer and Spencer, Competence at Work; and top performance and leadership competence studies published in Richard H. Rosier (ed.), The Competency Model Handbook, Volumes One and Two (Boston : Linkage, 1994 and 1995), Much of the material that follows comes from Working with Emotional Intelligence by Daniel Goleman (Bantam, 1998), and The Emotionally Intelligent Workplace by Goleman and Cherniss

---

Self-awareness is the ability to accurately sense and identify personal feelings, coupled with the ability to understand and evaluate them. Not only are you aware that they're there, but also you know what you do with them. To be fully aware of your feelings, you must not only identify them, but you must also acknowledge and accept them for what they are. Self-awareness is complete comprehension of your varying internal states, your likes and dislikes, what you have at your disposal in terms of your individual resources, your perceptions to new things, and your ability to feel a new emotion. As you become more self-aware, you'll be able to trigger a more immediate response to your own feelings based on the arsenal of experiences that you've established as your "emotional bank account". Self-awareness is critical in achieving optimum success because not effectively being in touch with your own feelings can limit your overall effectiveness. Consider the previous discussion of the relationship between the limbic brain and the neocortex; feeling and emotion develops in one area but must be translated and communicated by another. If you're having certain apprehensive feelings about the way that a manager is behaving but are conflicted on the interpretation of those feeling and the appropriate response, as an employee, you will render yourself ineffective and begin to diminish your own value long before you ever become disgruntled.

Employees and managers with high self-awareness are able to conduct more honest and accurate performance reviews, which will be evident in a very thorough and often overly-critical self-assessment portion of the annual review. They'll welcome feedback, and to a large degree, enjoy it. As an employee being reviewed for promotion or a raise, you possess a higher degree of expectation management skills as you know exactly what you bring to the table. Self-aware employees have a certain self-confidence about them, a genuine authenticity in the what they say and how they communicate them. They perceive emotionally stressful situations accurately and objectively and are willing to take a risk when they believe that what they are doing is right. The self-aware employee is a valued employee and team member, as he understands the "why" of his feelings and can consistently make values-based decisions.

Self-Awareness
Self-awareness as a subset has three basic competencies within it, which are emotional self-awareness, accurate self-assessment, and overall self-confidence. Emotional self-awareness is the ability to recognize your own emotions and their effects. From the way you behave in response to social cues to the overall effect on workplace performance, the emotionally self-aware employee can understand feelings in terms of his probable behavioral response. Employees who are highly developed in this competency would generally be referred to as having strong "awareness" or the internal workings of the office and politics. They understand the connection between their feelings and what they actually do and say and can also answer the question as to "why" those feelings occur based on previous personal or professional experiences. They recognize how their feelings affect their work and team performance and are aware of how their core values and career goals play a role in how they manage their feelings.

Emotionally self-aware employees will be able to direct their feelings into the execution of their values-based career strategic plan. The second competency within self-awareness is an accurate self-assessment, or a process of identifying an individual's resources, abilities, and strengths and thereby acknowledging and accepting his limits. This is what many would refer to as the "reality check". It's based on the employee's desire to receive feedback in the spirit of continuous improvement and lifelong learning.

Understanding what you truly bring to the table in terms of talents and ability as well as how to reconcile that with your own goals and objectives will allow you to focus more intently on areas of your performance that require development long before you'll ever have to be directed to do so by any supervisor or manager. Self-confidence is an individual's own belief as an employee in his ability to accomplish what is asked of him. It's the firm conviction that everything in that job description that falls under your responsibility will be accomplished adequately (and more than often exceeded). It's your own acknowledgement and affirmation that you are the best person for that job. If this self-confidence is diminished, then there's no question that an employee will begin to have thoughts of departing for another organization, as he'll consistently feel defeated and will demonstrate a diminishing lack of focus. The need for self-confidence is a basic human need, as it relates directly to self-worth and esteem as defined in Maslow's Hierarchy of Needs. As Maslow described esteem as a "deficiency need", the lack of self-esteem and confidence in the workplace will result in an anxious and tense atmosphere. Self-confidence is the ability to present yourself in an assured, unhesitating manner with the courage to voice your views and opinions that may not always be popular in the workplace. If your values affirm that your thoughts are in alignment, then your self-confidence will allow you share your thoughts without fear of rejection. The emotionally self-aware employee is able to have the difficult conversations at the difficult times with confidence and without fear of organizational retaliation.

It takes courage to become truly self-aware, as you may have to admit that there are areas in which you're simply deficient. When coupled with a proven set of core values, self-awareness will pay dividends to the employee when he can align his intentions with action.

Self-Management

The second subset is self-management, which is the employee's ability to understand his emotions and use that understanding to turn situations to his benefit. It's not enough to be self-aware, knowing how to turn the awareness into action. The ability to use feelings to reason (which may sound contradictory, as many would assert that feelings aren't always reasonable) will intentionally create a values-based action. Enjoying a workplace that allows for actions that are consistent with values will lead directly to loyalty and an engaged experience. Self-management is critical to the workplace for managers and employees because when people are better at managing their emotions, they will inherently become more effective. Unregulated behavior stemming from misinterpreted emotions will create nothing but confusion for the employee as well as coworkers and will significantly hinder results. People who are good managers of their emotions are generally open to changes in policy and practice, as they know they'll have a conditioned response. They're effective in mood management, consistent in stress management, can be intentionally productive, and behave in a reasonable and rational way in times of crisis. One thing that's consistent across all organizations and industries is that things will change, people will change, and processes will evolve. Any time we experience change (whether we consciously admit it or not in terms of what we say or do), there is a level of discomfort and uncertainty that comes with it. Feelings of insecurity can begin to affect our workplace behavior unless we have the skillset to understand, interpret, and manage our feelings according to our accurate self-assessment.

The self-management subset has six basic competencies which allow for control and direction of thoughts and feelings. First is the overarching theme of emotional self-control, which is not "flying off the handle" when things don't go the expected or desired way in the workplace. Emotional self-control is the ability to curb a potentially negative or destructive impulse (think Andy Bernard punching a hole in wall in Season 3, Episode 14 of *The Office*) and bring clarity to contentious discussions.

FYI

"Flying off the handle" is a reference to the way a loose axe-head would be uncontrollably launched from the handle during motion, being potentially dangerous or even deadly.

Trustworthiness is maintaining standards of honesty and integrity and just go along even when it's easier emotionally not to do so. Trustworthy employees will often communicate their intentions, ideas, and feelings openly and honestly and will welcome the same honesty in return. When your values are clear, your choices will be easy; and you will be able to confront unethical actions and decisions from others with confidence. Conscientiousness is taking responsibility for personal performance and is not playing the "blame game" when it comes time for a difficult conversation about where you've actually performed compared to where you believed you performed. Any employee who is strong in self-awareness, however, will already know this type of conversation is coming long before it ever occurs. The complaining behavior that is often exhibited by employees advancing in the negativity cycle is a direct detractor of an emotionally intelligent workplace as it diminishes the responsibility of employees to remain conscientious. Adaptability is the employee's ability to shift responsibilities and functions quickly without delay in productivity, as their values and interpretation of them should remain consistent. This is not the same as learning new skillsets to perform completely different job but more of a reference to quickly changing priorities in the workplace. As dynamics continue to change, being able to rapidly adapt to those changes and continue to perform, because you've got a firm handle on your emotions, will continuously lead you to success and recognition when you avoid problems and maintain effectiveness.

Optimism is the old adage describing the difference between an optimist and a pessimist in that the "optimist sees the donut, the pessimist the hole." Optimism leads to seeing the good in other employees and in the situations at hand, even when disagreement surrounding the origins of those situations from time to time arise. As human beings, we're conditioned to want to solve problems and identify flaws. In many companies, this is the basis of progress and profitability (i.e. Lean Six Sigma and Toyota Production System). There is merit to intentionally focusing on separating the analytical problem-solving nature of a job to the relationship side of the workplace, as it detracts from a healthy environment if relationships are dissected with the same "waste-elimination" approach to a task. The employees who can forcibly invoke optimism at times will see "opportunities" more than "threats" and have positive expectations about change. Optimism allows the employee to think about the future in terms of the results as opposed to the obstacles on the road to success. Initiative is the individual ability to decide, communicate, and act on a problem. People who have initiative are consistently striving to improve, to take on more, to experience new challenges, and ultimately to find new levels of success. Initiative will often reward those who have the courage to be first in action and innovation.

All competencies within self-management can be further developed with intentional effort. Try going through your work week and making a list of all of the difficulties that you encountered during each day. Aside from the results, consider the interactions with coworkers or managers that contributed to the difficulty. How did you respond physically and mentally? What would you have said differently if you could have the conversation again? Was there a more effective solution that you didn't consider then but have since determined? If the timing is still appropriate, try and revisit the difficult moments with those who were involved, as it will further your behavioral conditioning to talk through the areas that were difficult for you and will provide some closure to those areas that may be unsettled. If not, consider the alternatives you discovered, and conceptually commit to implementing process changes to close the gaps between what was desired and what was actually accomplished in the next opportunity.

Social Awareness

Social awareness, as the third subset EI refers to how employees participate in work relationships and perceive other's feelings, needs, and concerns. This is where the EI transitions from being a self-focus skill to the ability to recognize and appropriately respond to the emotions and feelings of others (assuming that you're still engaged enough in the workplace to care). This is where we really get into the concept of making friends instead of adding them in the workplace and inspiring instead of manipulating. As people need to have a sense of belonging, the place where most adults spend the majority of their day should be conducive to engaging one another through acceptance. Social acceptance stems from an emotionally intelligent culture. Social awareness has three basic competencies: empathy, organizational awareness, and service orientation.

Empathy is the experience of understanding other people's thoughts, feelings, and concerns. This differs from sympathy in that you're not just feeling sorry for them; you're feeling what they're feeling. People with empathy are able to constantly pickup on emotional cues from their coworkers and respond appropriately, for they can appreciate not only what people are saying but why they are saying it. This is where the "start with why" mentality goes to a slightly deeper level, as the empathetic employee is challenged to interpret the "what" in order to console the "why". Empathy doesn't always refer to something sad or emotionally charged but can also refer to the ability to relate to people from different backgrounds and cultures as their values may significantly differ from yours. Empathy doesn't imply agreement, only understanding. It's the ability to feel what another person feels and respond accordingly with sincerity, as opposed to a rapid-fire textbook answer. Empathy is the key to taking a workplace relationship a little bit further than what exists in the reporting procedures in any type of organizational chart, as it is the competency that will pay a coworker the ultimate compliment, a validation of his perspective. Empathy is difficult to display if it's not innate, but it *can* be learned through intentional focus on non-verbal cues and behaviors so that it provides perspective to the "why" behind the "what" of the verbiage.

Organizational awareness is the ability to understand the existing relationships in your company or organization as well as those relationships' effect on getting business done. Who are the real decision makers, and who can influence them? It's not about manipulation here as much as it is about influence and recognizing values and cultures of organizations and how they affect the way that people act and behave. This is the ability to assess the political nature of your workplace and how to thrive (or survive) in it. It's unfortunate that this component to social awareness isn't normally achieved until you've been in a workplace for quite some time because the insight gained through becoming organizationally aware will prevent a great deal of disappointment. Now, it's a very real possibility that this level of organizational awareness is what has led you to recognize that you're in a toxic culture, as you learn to perceive the way business is done is in conflict with your values. If that is the case, then congratulations for having developed the organizational awareness to make that type of realization because it will only sharpen your ability to evaluate your next environment at a more efficient rate and provide you with more questions to ask up front in evaluating the company's culture. If you're considering working for a family business, this component will not only be important but critical in understanding the power players in terms of organizational effectiveness. You'll need to quickly gain insight to who has influence and authority based on things such as last name, tenure with the organization, and access to the boss. I mention the family business structure specifically because the transition from a corporate structure with a robust HR system to the make-up-the-rules-as-we-go mentality that often lives within the family business has proven difficult for many employees.

The third social awareness competency is service orientation, which is all about your role in helping others meet their needs. This one's a little bit more difficult, especially if you have the mentality that you're there to do the job that you are hired to do, nothing more and nothing less. The service orientation directly creates alignment with your coworkers as you focus not only on your efforts, but on theirs. The reaction that they have to those efforts will provide you with an in-depth look of how your colleagues show appreciation, show signs of support, and offer feedback. A service-oriented mindset will allow for some "quick wins" in the first few weeks of employment with your new company, as you'll gain a reputation as a team player (even if you're not). As an employee, and possibly as a friend in the future if these relationships continue to develop, your social-awareness is going to be continually important as it will provide insight to your authenticity and perception of value in the organization.

Social Skills

When you're sending emotional signals, receiving them, and then implementing the self-awareness and self-management tactics that control the message in which you respond, the emotional intelligence is coming together. Social skills is the fourth subset and probably one of the most misused terms in popular culture. Generally, you'll hear someone who has a hard time acting appropriately in public referred to as having "no social skills". In fact, all individuals possess the social competencies; they just practice varying degrees of development. Communication in different settings is certainly a component but is only one competency in a collection of attributes designed to support positive interactions. The employee who is highly competent in social skills is the employee whom others would describe as an "all around good guy", as most interactions conducted with this individual leave them feeling positive. These are the competencies that will be most readily identifiable because they're quickly perceived as they're designed to be projected externally. As you progress through this list, think about the most enjoyable leadership experiences that you've had and who you've worked with in your life and career. Try and recall specific examples of their leadership style and what they were bringing to the table in terms of these competencies.

Developing others is the ability to promote long-term learning and development through a "what can I do for you?" approach. It focuses on employee development in terms of the individual's intended outcome as opposed to a formal method of teaching or training skills. This type of management or coworker takes personal interest in you, the employee. This coworker is generally the one who makes the time to get to know you and what you want to accomplish, even when it's not his job to do so. They'll do this by spending more time discussing current performance and offering advice and insights on what you can do to progress in the organization.

Inspirational leadership is the ability to bring people together to get a job done. These folks build a strong sense of belonging within the group and lead others to feel that they are a part of something bigger than themselves, even when they're not the stronger player. If someone is on a team, and it's clear that their professional competencies or skill sets are not as developed when compared to some of the other individuals, they still walk away feeling as if they made a significant contribution - the inspirational leadership competency was at its peak.

Influence is the ability to persuade, convince, or impact others to get them to support your goals and ideas not because you want them to but because they firmly believe that it's the right thing to do. Influence can be power and takes a proven track record of trust and results to establish. Your investment in relationships will lead to your escalation as an influential person, and the loss of trust in a relationship will certainly degrade influence to a possibly irreparable degree.

Communication is the ability to send clear messages and signals to an audience in an effective manner. Those with adept social skills have a variety of communication mechanisms that they can utilize from time to time based on the needs of their audience. Verbal or non-verbal, written or oral, the intense focus on receiving (listening) in addition to sending is hallmark in building trust and influence through communication. Through the ability to "pull" information in addition to "pushing" information will encourage open and honest dialogue with management and coworkers.

Conflict management is the ability to handle difficult individuals, groups, problems, or tense situations with the utmost discretion and professionalism and is a clear indicator of social competence. Managers who are often promoted to a supervisory position for the first time without any formal training will struggle in conflict management because they will generally default to the skill sets that they have seen as they've developed. Human resources professionals will agree that the field of conflict management and resolution has developed significantly over the years and has evolved from the simple "win-lose" decision. This competency encourages transparent debates, open discussions, and honest dialogue with a win-win mentality. The highly skilled individual in conflict management can bring everyone to the table and address a conflict or problem head-on, resulting in everyone walking away with a feeling of accomplishment.

The building-bonds competency is demonstrated by intentionally going out of one's way to take the professional side of a relationship to a more personal friendship based on trust and respect. Employees who transition jobs and companies frequently find benefit in developing and using this skill set, as each job change is an opportunity to grow their network. Each new task or assignment is an opportunity to grow and expand personal connections which will be maintained for years. This is a competency that I personally value because every job I've ever had has come as a result of learning of the company from someone in my network.

Collaboration is about working cooperatively with others and serving on a team, even when it's not the most convenient thing to do. Putting competition aside for the good of the project or result promotes a friendly and cooperative atmosphere that encourages participation. In a collaborative environment, a group of individuals with different backgrounds, experiences, skill sets, and ideas can come together and somehow form a collaborative team all moving forward to share plans, information, and resources in pursuit of common goal. It is through this pursuit that the team of individuals forms an identity in a collective movement which will bind them together beyond the project.

The competencies that fall under social skills are the basic skills that every emotionally intelligent employee must understand and employ to maximize effectiveness in the workplace; these attributes of social competence will be universal, regardless of the organization. Now, revisit your most enjoyable leadership experience. From the previous descriptors, where was your leader effective? Socially skilled employees will create experiences where their interactions will be remembered not for what they say but how they made the other person feel. It's highly likely that your most enjoyable leadership experience had you feeling pretty great. The targeted development of these competencies through self- awareness and management will allow your emotional intelligence to pave the way for stronger and more genuine workplace relationships.

Real Relationships Lead to Real Engagement

The concepts of a strong relationship aren't going to change, only the individuals and the applications. Understanding the fundamentals of what makes an emotionally intelligent employee and making a concerted effort to develop how you perceive, understand, address, and manage your own emotions internally and externally will serve as the catalyst in strengthening your company culture. As your EI continues to expand, you'll begin to pass on your knowledge and abilities to others and contribute to a cultural shift towards a significantly more engaging employee experience. The manner in which you interact with other people will fundamentally improve through discovery and interpretation of your emotions and will provide valuable insight into what type of employee you really are and what type of employee you intend to be at your next workplace

Chapter Seven
It's Toxic, You're Slipping Under

Take Home Message:

- A shift in values has led to a rise in cultural toxicity across organizations, leading to a poor company culture becoming the primary reason for employee departures

- Chronic stress with little time for employee recuperation is the most common trait among organizations described as toxic by departing employees

- Key indicators of immature and inexperienced leadership are managing outside of scope, poor hiring decisions, unreasonable expectations, conflict avoidance, poor communication, dysfunctional relationships, and a lack of sound decision making

- Recognizing the signs of toxicity will better prepare the employee for transitioning into a new work environment with clearer expectations for a healthy employment relationship

Tom Smykowski: Have you seen this? I knew it! I knew it! [he hands them a piece of paper]

Michael Bolton: What? It's the staff meeting. So what?

Tom Smykowski: So what? We're all screwed, that's what! They're gonna downsize Initech.

Samir: What are you talking about Tom? How do you know that?

Tom Smykowski: How do I know? They're bringing in a consultant, that's how I know. That's what this staff meeting is all about! It happened at Initrode last year. You have to interview with this consultant, they call in efficiency experts. But what you're really doing is interviewing for your own job!

Michael Bolton: Tom, every week you say you're gonna lose your job and you're still here.

Tom Smykowski: Not this time. I'll bet I'm the first one laid off! Just the thought of having to go to the state unemployment office and stand in line with those scumbags!

Office Space is to the white collar employee as *This Is Spinal Tap* is to the musician. Through the satirical recreation of the worst parts of every American employee's job, *Office Space* allowed viewers to live through the eyes of the employee who was able to mentally escape the toxic corporate culture.

The emotionally inept boss, Bill Lumbergh, who asks a lot but delivers very little; the mild mannered and mostly-ignored Milton; the loyal friends and colleagues; and the oh-so popular efficiency experts come in to ask some questions and immediately spark the idea of potential downsizing. Now, since all of us can't escape our increasingly toxic work environments through occupational hypnotherapy like Peter Gibbons, we are forced to find other ways to deal with our toxic work environments or get out of them before someone decides to burn down the building. In all fairness, Milton did give an adequate warning in blatantly pointing out that his red Swingline stapler was inappropriately taken.

The fact is that we recognized that we were unhappy as employees, but as we've examined ourselves and our behavior as potential root causes, it's now time to take a look at the organization and discuss the top tell-tale sign of a toxic culture. While the Grammy-winning song by Britney Spears makes the idea of toxicity sound somewhat intriguing, when it comes to the workplace, there's nothing sexy and seductive about it. You're not quitting because the job is too hard; you're quitting because it's no longer worth it. We all began our careers and current jobs in a similar fashion, as we probably exited the interview process being offered the position with a great deal of excitement. That excitement manifested itself into enthusiasm for the first few days, and maybe even weeks, that we were on the job. We had a certain zeal about us as we approached tasks and were determined to make our mark. As time went on and we began to get more familiar with the environment and orient ourselves to the way things were done, that enthusiasm declined into indifference. Indifference eventually became concern with the way that things were being handled, concern with management, concern with colleagues, and concern with the overall culture. That concern eventually became disappointment. Disappointment led to disengagement, and disengagement is leading to the eventual departure.

Trends of Toxicity

The question is, throughout our time with the organization and what we witnessed throughout the rise of this toxic workplace, what exactly did we see that led us to this point? What causes a workplace to become contaminated anyway? What are some signs that we saw and can know to look for in the future before we get into another toxic professional relationship? Reflecting on the previous source of discontent will allow us to get into the "why" of cultural toxicity and gain the skill set to evaluate our next career move with a more experienced point of view. There's been a lot of things that have changed in the United States of America over the past couple of decades: we've seen a shift in values to some degree, which has also played a part in workplace culture. The common workplace has almost become resonant of a dysfunctional family; there are certain actions that go on behind closed doors that people just don't like to talk about in public. There's certain chaos that arises from multiple points of stress. There are stresses that lead to poor decision-making and poor decision-making that leads to dissatisfaction, disengagement, and departure of those who felt the effects.

Bottom line: Values that may have once been foundational to a workplace (values that may have even been brought up and discussed at length in your interview process) are now a distant memory in terms of organizational priority. The organization now is damaging, destructive, and sometimes even unbearable to the employee. There's no one reason for workplaces moving in a toxic direction. Economically, things are getting more and more difficult for businesses (especially the smaller family businesses) to survive and to compete. Any time you inject economic stress or financial hardship on even the strongest of values-driven organizations, there will certainly be some degree of a shift in behavior. Personal agendas that work their way into the overall management and leadership structure can begin to take over the way that decisions are made and relationships are handled.

Personal agendas and poorly managed relationships will ultimately lead to conflict, which will drive a very decisive wedge in between the employees and management at every level within the organizational chart and begin to erode loyalty. Inevitably, all of these factors and more can inject tension into the workplace, ultimately evolve into emotional issues, create emotional disarray, and disconnect the employee from his job and workplace. When the employee begins to observe signs of an unhealthy relationship emerging, he will begin to contemplate making the decision to get out and usually get out quickly. Throughout the evolution of the toxic workplace there have been several consistencies amongst all environments (regardless of industry) that employees cite for reasons they deemed the workplace "not safe" for work. The close-knit businesses we used to know and love for their healthy values such as community, integrity, cooperation, loyalty, honesty, inclusiveness, trust, and teamwork have been replaced by nepotism and the often times soulless materialism that accompanies it: status-seeking, egocentrism, exploitation, manipulation, reckless hiring decisions, manipulation, and aggression. All words used above were taken from the publicly available exit reviews of a select group of companies. Do any of those sound familiar?

In 2005, 21% of US workers made voluntary job changes according to a *Harris* interactive poll, citing the top reason for departing was the lack of opportunity for personal growth and earnings potential, followed closely by time off and flexibility, financial compensation, culture and work environment, benefits, and the relationship with the supervisor. In 2015, the same poll was conducted and concluded that the number one reason for employees making voluntary job changes was the "corporate culture and management climate", followed by lack of empowerment, internal politics, lack of recognition, inflexibility in schedule, and lack of benefits came in as important to only 3%. The primary reasons that employees leave has observed a shift from a very unemotional, black-and-white policy and structure-driven decision to a very emotionally-invested one based on the work environment and the feelings that the employee encounters on a daily basis.

Ten Toxic Indicators

There are ten common indicators of a toxic work environment which you may have seen or encountered. These will now be discussed in detail. Please keep in mind that an organization does not need to display more than one or show all of these to become too toxic to be productive because toxicity is a very subjective measure to every employee. Toxicity is a driving force of an employee's state of mind from a point of enthusiasm and excitement to a point of disengagement and departure.

Chronic Stress

The number one toxic component to any workplace or job site is described as a chronic level of high stress. The work will maintain at a certain level of intensity for ongoing degrees and lengths of time without any significant room to recuperate. There's very little of what employees would consider downtime or time to catch their breath. Stress can be caused by a variety of different factors that have been discussed previously: financial or economic hardships, disagreement in hiring decisions, poor human resources policy, the presence of nepotism, or the overall management culture: anything that has led employees to feel that they must work harder than they are physically, mentally, or emotionally capable of in order to get the job done. When emotionally intelligent leadership is in place, measures will be taken to reduce the stress and level the workload. When something is not injected to disrupt the stress, such as new leadership, new direction from a competent board of directors, or outside guidance from a consultant, then the continuity of a stressful environment will prove to be the undoing of the organization through the departure of potentially engaging and capable employees. As every employee handles stress differently, the importance is on the emotionally intelligent leader and coworker to observe and interpret signs of a stressed employee and take action to provide support. Some employees deal with stress by complaining, while others will internalize the stress until it is beyond repair, and the employment relationship is now terminal.

Immature Leadership

The second sign of a toxic environment, and one that continues to make its way to the top of the exit interview charts as the primary reason for employee departure, is "immature leadership" and "inexperienced management". I think that most of us (myself included) have had our share with multiple levels of one or the other or both simultaneously. Leadership and management are considerably different fields which can be mutually exclusive. It's nice when competence in both areas comes together, but they certainly don't have to. If toxic workplaces are fueled by stress, then they're driven by immature and dysfunctional leaders. From the board room to the break room, every organization is built with certain number of "influencers", either by position or by evolution. When those influencers are in formal leadership positions and have developed toxic behaviors, the effects of the behaviors will be amplified and have the ability to disrupt, disorganize, and destroy the organization in which they are in place to serve. Immature leadership may demonstrate some characteristics synonymous with a lack of developed emotional intelligence. Poor feedback practices, inadequate communication, unprofessional relationships and favoritism, impulsiveness, and varying degrees of self-control will point employees nowhere but out the door.

Immature leadership practices can be observed when employees notice a trend of managing entities operating out of scope. This is where an uninformed and immature board of directors can come into an organization with the mindset of a group of CEOs, as opposed to collective body of voting members entrusted with the organizational strategy. When a board tries to micromanage daily operations, that puts not only the individual contributor (who likely understands the reporting structure and the role of the board of directors) but especially the chief executive who's trying to run operations on a tactical front in a conflict state of decision making. Board members who are trying to work directly with staff members and leaving the chief executive out of the loop will create a large amount of confusion amongst all roles and responsibilities. When the CEO tries to do the job of the middle manager or the front line employee, as opposed to implementing strategic direction of the board, it will also lead to organizational confusion. Whenever leadership fails to create (or allows by a micromanaging board) a culture of navigating outside of clearly defined roles and responsibilities in the spirit of "doing more", then confusion is inevitable. Confusion leads to chaos, and chaos will be a stress contributor to disengagement.

The solution for this potential issue is insuring that all members of leadership and management understand clearly and presently their roles and responsibilities. From an individual board member, to the chairman, to the chief executive officer, to the individual contributor, and even the contracted temporary employee, a culture of responsibility and accountability within designated areas of operation will alleviate out-of-scope operations. There may also be a case of a pure misunderstanding of employees' responsibilities. Managers occasionally develop patterns of having their "go-to" employees for certain things, even when it's not (or no longer) their job. This may be based on a personal relationship or a previous working relationship, but it can create a lack of clarity in job performance as it relates to job requirements, especially when it's time for performance reviews. For instance, if an employee is hired in the accounts payable department and masters the AP management system but transfers into Human Resources after a few years, no components of the AP job should transfer with the employee regardless of how convenient it may be. This sets the employer up for failure if there's ever a dispute regarding job performance and the competencies required for it. This all happens because of a manager's oversight and inadvertent managing outside of the employee scope of responsibility.

Inexperienced managers consistently try hiring personnel outside of a conventional hiring process out of convenience because they "need somebody yesterday!". This also extends to a board of directors who is searching for a chief executive. When hiring decisions are made on a timeline without regard to a values-based process in order to "get someone in there" to continue operations and sign the checks, this can not only lead to bad hires but will also create some discomfort in the organization as employees observe the actions of the leaders and directors as they bring in a potential colleague or a boss.

Unreasonable expectations for productivity and goal accomplishment for managers or employees, especially when there is a head count shortage, can create disproportionate workloads across the labor force. When organizations are in a cost-saving mode, they may enter into a hiring freeze. When automatic assumption is to level the remaining load amongst all the existing employees without strategic regard to their individual strengths, disengagement is on the horizon as employees will only be able to physically and mentally produce so much for so long. Hiring freezes or reductions in force with a clearly communicated timeline will provide a mental roadmap for the remaining team and will establish a targeted approach to a return to normalcy.

Immature leaders will often avoid conflict. They may be good at directing but not necessarily at relating. Trying to engage an immature leader-manager into a conversation regarding what is simply "not working" for the employee in the workplace may lead to a dead-end or an unproductive conversation best summarized as a waste of time. The basis for their inability to have crucial and difficult conversations is representative of their difficulty showing empathy and support. They expect their employees to come in and give as much as they do themselves. You may have a leader-manager who is first into work every day and last out but is not necessarily the most mature in the way that he's running the business; however, he expects that if he's there, then you're there. Because hey, it's what works for him. That emotionally unintelligent application is a key indicator of a lack of experience in personnel management, as individual contributors often have found a methodology that "works for them". Mature leaders understand that there is no universal method for productivity and adding value.

Poor communication up, down, and sideways is a clear indicator that certain leader-managers do not possess the skill set in which to relate to multiple employees in the way that they'd like to or need to be spoken to. There's a lot of talk across organizations about the golden rule, which is "treat people the way that you want to be treated". However, there's a book that came out several years ago by Tony Alessandra and Michael O'Connor, both PhDs, that's introduces *The Platinum Rule*. The Platinum Rule, for all intents and purposes, is the employee saying, "Know me well enough to know how I'd like to be told." That is the basis of effective communication from a leader-manager in the workplace. From subordinate to colleague to superior, the means of communication should be tailored to fit those in which the communication is intended. High aggression, intimidation, bullying, instilling fear into others as opposed to motivating action are very archaic types of management communication that were formerly predominant in retail and military-esque environments as opposed to the more emotionally intelligent communication styles of the 21st century. Depending on the generation of your manager, you may be seeing some remnants of these techniques.

All of these components that have been described above are often underlined by a lack of sound decision making skills. The ability to make a sound and rational decision is one that is most questioned by disgruntled employees, as failure to do so contributes to a lack of trust for their senior leadership. Immature leaders and inexperienced managers are the often least trusted members of a contemporary work team, for they fail to create the emotional connection with the employees for whom they are entrusted to care and develop. As previously mentioned, where there is no trust, there is no loyalty, and a lack of loyalty certainly progresses to a rapid departure by employees.

Dysfunctional Relationships

The third key indicator of a toxic work environment is a surplus of dysfunctional relationships and dysfunctional dynamics such as cliquishness, complete with company insiders and outsiders. Individuals who have been around since the organization started will often times lead the pack, and anybody else who comes in will have to earn the right to sit at their lunch table. Often times, these are people who have been moved into senior positions but aren't necessarily leaders. In the case that someone new comes into the organization and assumes the roles and responsibilities of one of the original "insiders", it may be quite some time (if ever) before the new person measures up to the person who was in the seat. The bitterness may be palatable, but if the new employee isn't receiving the information that he needs from other team members in the spirit of "loyalty" to their former colleague, then it will create an internal conflict. This behavior, if not addressed and discussed, will prove to be detrimental for developing and retaining top-tier talent in any organization that hopes to sustain.

Nepotism is a relationship driver that can be especially concerning when referring to the "family business." An organization would like to say that it promotes the most innovative, productive, or visionary workers to the top of their leadership ranks, which may be the case. It's likely to be the case in developed organizations where the possibility for nepotism isn't readily available. The dangers of nepotism in an organizational culture are certainly ones that should be discussed and not overlooked, but if you're not within the family structure, then it's understandable that this may be quite a controversial and uncomfortable issue to discuss with your employers.

One of the most common issues with family businesses when nepotism is a factor in driving employees out is a perceived distortion of workplace fairness. Workers will become dissatisfied because they believe with some degree of certainty that they will never quite measure up in a way that will propel them to a certain level of senior leadership, thus engagement will be directly proportional. Employees will have less incentive to perform their responsibilities diligently and to the best of their ability if they feel that their path to promotion is going to be undermined by which member of the boss's family wants to be closer to the flag pole. A company that employs such tactics should realize that it will disengage some potential top-producing employees, for human nature drives them towards achievement and promotion. If nothing else, workers are going to complain in one form or another if they feel that they are slighted when compared to a family member who may not be as talented. The overall loss of productivity that nepotism will usually lead to will hopefully allow the ranking member of the family to realize that some decisions must be made to ensure top talent are given a clear path to organizational growth and development. Employees who are rewarded and promoted solely because of their relationships with management are likely to be under qualified for the positions that they're expected to move in to, which can lead to an erosion of leadership skills at the top and the demoralization of more deserving, more qualified, and often times more competent candidates. Some organizations will have anti-nepotism policies because they realize the danger of having an environment where favoritism plays a role in deciding who makes it to the top, but many organizations choose not to go that direction, assuming that it will never happen to them. Nepotism is frustrating and disheartening for some top performers, but where corporate structures may prevent this practice by policy, the family business often has the flexibility to reward its trusted agents in ways prohibited by more stringent corporate structures.

Further attributes of dysfunctional relationships can be insincere communication with employees by saying one thing and acting another. Moreover, backstabbing and environments where co-workers, middle managers, senior leadership, and employees feel that they need to go against one another from time to time is rooted once again in a lack of trust.

Low Employee Morale- The Cultural Thermometer

A fourth indicator of a toxic work environment is a simple assessment of employee morale. Low morale of yourself and your fellow employees will be manifested in your overall mood when you come into work. You may get up and start your day excited with your family, but from the time that you walk out the door and eventually get to work, you'll find that your mood actually declines and your anxiety is on the rise. As a result, there's little enthusiasm or joy in what you do on a daily basis.

Reflection: How full is your bucket?

Tom Rath and Donald Clifton authored the book *How Full is Your Bucket?* to illustrate the effect of positive and negative interactions in our life through the metaphor of a dipper and a bucket. When our bucket is full, we feel great; when it's not, we feel terrible. Thinking through the below questions with regard to your workplace, how full is your bucket after filling or dipping from it based on how your response makes you feel?

How often do you find that you experience true and genuine happiness in the job that you do? What does your workplace currently do to encourage a higher morale? How often does the boss, or supervisor, or fellow employees get together to intentionally do things outside of the office with the intent to increase employee morale? Are there bonus or incentive programs, even if they're directly monetary in nature? Are there things to give employees incentives to perform on a higher level to incentivize your contribution or to at least keep your inputs and production interesting to you on a personal level.

Disregard for Employee Work-Life Balance

Fifth, is a company with no clear and present regard (or even acknowledgment) for the importance of a work-life balance. The organization does not want to enjoy your company but presents itself as wanting to "own" you in terms of ensuring it has top-of-mind status in all of your waking hours. You may work more than 40 hours per week on a regular basis (which may be fine for a while), and you may have seen what was once a social life dwindle into a "nice to have" as opposed to a regular occurrence when it comes to the way that you spend your time. You feel as if you have to choose between essentially keeping your job, which you don't like, and having some sort of a personal life. You perceive that your manager doesn't really view you as a human being but as an individual there for one reason and one reason alone: production. Your requests for an increased head count may continue to get denied because, after all, you're getting the job done. Employees must evaluate their true return on this investment. Feeling that they are contributing to something greater and working alongside a great team of people will only sustain an employee's personal satisfaction for so long, as the disregard for a healthy and consistent work-life balance will lead to employees' rapid departure, especially in a contemporary workplace society that is moving more and more flexible in terms employee geo-location.

Unreasonable Expectations

Number six in the list of common toxic trends is unreasonable expectations. If you are put in a situation or an environment with goals set at such a degree that you perceive the organization almost expects you to fail, then your movement from enthusiasm to indifference will accelerate. Following any common goal setting methodology will attest that the goals for employees should be reasonably attainable with a realistic target for completion. The lack of a realistic expectation of success will demoralize employees, even to a degree of not ever reaching maximum effort. When workload and expectations are unreasonable for one person's accomplishment, a clear message is sent regarding the organization's priority on meeting the employee's need for value and utility.

Loyalty is an Option, not an Expectation

The seventh toxic trait is the perspective that loyalty is nice to have but not a must-have. On your first day at work, many human resources departments will have you acknowledge with your signature that they are an "at-will employer". Basically, the at-will employment agreement will present language discussing the law and the reason that it's in place. But what the organization is telling you at your very first administrative experience after the hiring process is complete is that the bottom line is, if we're ready to sever this relationship and part ways as employer and employee, then we can do so at any time and for any reason. Knowing that your relationship can be so potentially temporary and ended so quickly without much of a discussion or review will certainly not go very far in getting you to invest all of your time, energy, and emotions into an organization that just reminded you that "if we want to terminate you, we will." You've effectively been told that you're not in a permanent relationship with your employer (you're just going to date for a while), which can subconsciously set the stage for a relationship built of limited loyalty and trust. Granted, at-will works both ways, but there's a certain degree of tact that can be employed to frame this in a way that doesn't sound so temperamental.

Weakened Human Resources Footprint

If the human resources department is viewed by leadership as an administrative facilitator rather than a strategic partner, then your workplace is potentially toxic due to the ongoing progression the human resources field. A weakened or non-existent human resources structure is the eighth toxic trait. Human resources is not just the part of an organization that will move a stack of papers from one pile to another in the spirit of efficiency but the department that bears the responsibility to recruit, retain, and promote great people in greater environments. Full-cycle human resource departments develop relationships with employees from pre-hire to retire and serve as the employee's unbiased outlet and "trusted agent" in discussing organizational behaviors and climate. When a strong Human Resources department is in place, employees feel a built-in system of support in their employment experience.

Inadequate Employee-Training Structure

Ninth is when performance expectations are high, maybe even unreasonable as previously discussed, yet training requirements are low. Employees may be expected to intuitively know what's expected from them without explanation and without support in terms of a curriculum designed to provide the outline to achieving success. Step-by-step guides and direction sets for each task will ensure a universal platform for job accomplishment and success as well as having individual training plans in place for each new employee. Employees often attribute failure in the job to a lack of comprehensive training or mentorship, which is easily addressed through development of complete training plans for each job. This eliminates the possibility of employees "never being told" how to perform a task. An organization cannot expect employees to perform without saying with certainty that they have been given every possible opportunity to succeed in the task, which comes from a robust training and development program for job performance as well as career progression. Consider how your current organization equipped you for job success based on the training in place upon your arrival. Did they ensure that you have everything you needed to perform your job safely and effectively?

Top-Down Communication

The final indicator of cultural toxicity we'll cover is when an organization thrives on information push without regard to information pull. There may be surveys and feedback that are regimented, maybe on a quarterly or annual basis, but communication from the bottom up is not often considered. When it is solicited, it may be viewed as a mandatory exercise to "check the box" as opposed to a genuine opportunity for input on the direction of the organization from the perspective of an employee who works on the front lines. Disregard for this sort of opinion may have been widely understood and practiced in the seventies and early eighties but has since been inverted in terms of the importance placed on employee opinions. In businesses that have engaged employees, one common factor that will tie many of them together is the need and utilization of employee feedback. This sort of bottom-up communication is what's known as information "pull". When information is pulled from the ground up to the top, as opposed to pushed from the top to the bottom in pursuit of compliance, engaged employees will continue to find new and creative ways to innovate, inspire, and contribute to the business that they're beginning to feel a part of.

Addressing Toxicity at Any Level

Amongst those 10 different telltale signs of a toxic work environment, you may have seen anywhere from one to as many as all 10 in your current environment. Any one of those for any one person may be enough to get you out the door. Depending on who you are and the degree of toxicity that you're dealing with, there are multiple options for you to address them. It may be apparent after considering the factors presented that you've reached a point that you're past trying to repair anything but your self-esteem and confidence. Perhaps, you're not an executive director, or CEO, or even a front line manager who has the ability to influence positive changes. If not, then consider bringing in an independent consultant to look at the organization and evaluate the way that you're conducting businesses.

Understanding the employees' role in creating a positive customer experience, Ford Motor Company deployed a team of consumer experience coaches to go into their dealership environments in order to get to know the employees and possibly recommend some changes in the spirit of progress. This is a practice that could be beneficial across multiple fronts, as there's a great deal of resources that can be called upon to detoxify the organization and possibly save and retain its higher contributors.

Regardless of your hierarchical level within your organization, you may not feel that you have the influence to make a difference, or maybe you've tried before and failed. If your suggestions for improvement continue to fall on deaf ears, then your best choice is to find a healthier workplace and to find a healthier workplace as soon as possible. Knowing what you know about a toxic culture and its effects on employees, you know that you don't want to experience that again. It can be tricky not to fall back into the same trap as you apply and pursue new jobs because most hiring managers will make their organization sound great as you're going through the hiring process. Try to gather some information about your upcoming organization's track record in terms of employee engagement. Connect with a few individuals on LinkedIn or other professional networking sites to get some initial feedback into what the organization is actually like once you're on the inside. By asking questions up front and finding a trusted agent who can share with you some initial insight, you'll be far less disappointed once you arrive and begin to perceive signs of a toxic culture. Hopefully, with the information and experience you've gained, the detailed indicators of a toxic environment will aid you in your pursuit to avoid repeating the past on your pathway to an engaging and fulfilling career.

Chapter Eight
Hasta La Vista: The Art of the Quit

Take Home Message:

- Preparation is the key to exiting a job efficiently and effectively

- Understanding of the current job market, personal finances, and company policies surrounding resignation should be obtained as part of an employee's exit strategy

- A well-organized and methodical resignation letter is a critical component to any departure

- More employees will remember the way you leave an organization as opposed to how you began

"Mr. Waturi, Frank. I quit…. I've been working here four and a half years. The work I did I probably could have done in six months. That leaves four years left over. Four years. If I had them now, like gold in my hand. Here, this is for you. Goodbye, DeDe. This life. Life, what a joke! This situation, this room. You look terrible, Mr. Waturi. You look like a bag of shit stuffed in a cheap suit. Not that anybody could look good under these zombie lights. I can feel them sucking the juice out of my eyeballs. Suck suck suck suck suck. $300 bucks a week. That's the news. For $300 bucks a week, I've lived in this sink, this used rubber. … Don't you think I know that, Frank? Don't you think I'm aware that there is a woman here? I can smell her, like a flower. I can taste her like sugar on my tongue. When I'm 20 feet away, I can hear the fabric of her dress when she moves in her chair. Not that I've done anything about it. I've gone all day, every day, not doing, not saying, not taking the chance, for $300 dollars a week. And Frank, the coffee, it stinks. It tastes like arsenic. These lights give me a headache. If they don't give you a headache, you must be dead, so let's arrange the funeral. You're not tellin' me nothin'. Why, I ask myself, why have I put up with you, I can't imagine. But I know. It's fear. Yellow freakin' fear. I've been too chickenshit afraid to live my life, so I sold it to you for $300 freakin' dollars a week! You are lucky I don't kill you! You're lucky I don't rip your freakin'

throat out! But I'm not going to! And maybe you're not so lucky at that. 'Cause I'm gonna leave you here, Mr. Waboo Waturi. And what could be worse than that? … DeDe?… How about dinner tonight?" –Tom Hanks as Joe Banks, *Joe Versus The Volcano*

Joe (Tom Hanks) makes the trek to his dead-end job making medical supplies every day and answering to his squeamishly unpleasant boss in a soul-sucking flickering florescent-lit office. He is sickly, weak, beaten down, and desperate for something new. A hypochondriac, Joe goes to doctors seeking for someone to tell him how to fix his life. One day, one doctor says, "You have a brain cloud." Well, that's the end for poor Joe, or so he thinks. With 6 months to live, he quits his job in the above high fashion but not before asking the pretty but mousy secretary (Meg Ryan) for dinner. The movie progresses as Joe is approached by Lloyd Bridges, who proposes that Joe become the willing human that the islanders of Waponi Woo sacrifice into an active volcano to appease angry gods. What a way to go out, right? I mean, who wouldn't want to deliver the pipe-bomb of a monologue on the ungrateful curators of the toxic organizations we're so eager to get out of?!

The Process of Quitting

There are multiple ways to go about delivering the final notification of departure to our current employers. But, before that happens, there's a few things that you should review like deciding what type of exit you'll eventually take before you reach the point of no return. Are you the humble and quiet, leave-your-letter-on-the-boss'-desk-on-a-Sunday-afternoon-so-he'll-see-it-first-thing-Monday-morning type of employee? Or, are you the more dramatic break-down-the-walls-of-the-quarterly-board-of-directors-meeting-with-both-guns-blazing-so-everyone-knows why-you're-on-your-way-out type?

Different Generations at Work

It's a unique time to examine the landscape of the contemporary workforce, as there are four different generations of employee currently contributing: the traditionalist, the Baby Boomer, the Generation Xer, and the Millennial. The reality is, of those four generations that are actively working right now, each of them looks at job transitioning and career fluctuation, a little bit differently. Depending on your generational classification as well as those you work with, your departure may be viewed a bit differently.

The traditionalists are the older individuals in the workforce right now (Born 1922-1944). They believe that job changing carries with it a stigma about being perceived as a "quitter". I was talking to a good friend of mine recently who's currently active duty in the United States military. He was talking about reviewing a resume' of an individual who had all of these great reviews coming in and just knew that he was going to get hired. He passed off the resume' to a "senior" individual in the organization, and the decision was made not to hire him because the individual had only averaged, in each job over the course of the last 12 years, about one year in each position. Given the perspective of the reviewer, this was seen as a negative. The traditionalist view is, "No way, this person's a quitter." Where the Millennial would say, "Look at all of the different experience that this guy's bringing to the table. We've got to move on this fast." The Baby Boomer (Born 1945-1961) would say that job changing puts you behind, that you're never actually going to quite advance if you continue to move around, which is true to some degree in some skilled professions, but for the most part that's beginning to evolve. Generation Xers (Born 1962-1981) understand that it's time, every once in a while, to move around and stay fresh through gaining a new perspective, and that lateral moves are sometimes a necessary part of enhancing your resume' as well as your skill sets. But, the epitome of embracing the job-change culture and the constant moving from one place to another lies in the Millennials (Born 1982-2000). If they're moving, they're growing, and if they're growing, then they're leading. Moving to the Millennial is like the cultural experience of visiting a foreign country; it's going to be something they just feel they have to do. Understanding some of the perspectives of the generations within your organization may provide some much needed insight into how your departure will be perceived and how to approach the crucial conversation. So, don't panic when it comes to actually making the decision to quit and walk out the door. Depending on what employer or hiring manager is looking at your resume', he is going to have a slightly different interpretation, yet understanding what that perspective is will take you one step further (at least psychologically) in the direction of that next interview process.

Considerations Before Departure

As excited as you are to finally be leaving the environment that's been weighing on your mind for quite some time, don't just think about the "getting out" factor of your current position. Think about some of the things that you'll be leaving behind, and reflect on why you decided to take this job in the first place. Remember what excited you about this company and organization. Remember the enthusiasm that was once present with you in this culture. No matter how unfulfilling or boring the current job has become, there were some good elements to it that led you to this position in the first place, and they should be given some thought and consideration before finally walking out the door and your official commitment to resigning.

It would be best to say that you should never resign without a firm commitment from another employer in hand; however, every situation is different based on the level of toxicity of your current organization. You may not have the luxury of waiting around for something better or even comparable. An important factor to keep in mind is to ensure that you're not just intending to offer your resignation in hopes that you're going to get a counteroffer from your current organization. If you desire to receive more compensation or a better benefit package out of the organization, then that's the conversation you should have, but fabrication of a better offer and the threat to resign in lieu of receiving an increase on your current organization is a very dangerous line to walk. If nothing else, your future advancement in the organization as well as your relationships will be put in jeopardy if it's ever discovered that your proposed counteroffer was fabricated; as a result, trust will most definitely diminish.

Your co-workers, superiors, and everyone involved may not all remember how you began your job- but they'll certainly remember how you'll leave it. It's going to create as much of an impression and will affect your overall reputation with the organization as much as (if not more than) any other results that you created. Quitting your job will likely be an emotional decision and situation. You may be sad or depressed a little bit. You may be angry with the decisions that the company has made and cannot wait for the opportunity to finally let it all out and let them know to what point your relationship has diminished. Or, you may be happy. All of which are emotional feelings that will affect this decision and will need to be expressed at exactly the right time and place and in the right manner.

Think about the intended outcome that you want your departure to have for you; think about the organization. Think about and your departure's role in the legacy that you're going to be leaving behind. Regardless of the reason, or multiple reasons, that you're leaving; resigning your position is a process and not just a one-time single action. If you're extremely angry and upset, ensure that you give yourself some time to consider that this move is the right decision, and it's not purely an angry emotion rearing its ugly head as the result of a retaliatory act for some injustice that you perceive. If you're elated about a new job opportunity that you've locked on to, then try not to gloat and brag or create any discontent or jealousy in the organization if it can be avoided. Finally, please acknowledge that too often your reasons for wanting to leave are not going to be resolved within a few months, and if it's possible to take some more time and think about how the organization and your overall reputation will benefit from doing so, then take as much time as you need. Odds are that the environment is not going anywhere, and you're the commodity that's at stake.

The Checklist to Quitting

Now if it is time, here's the checklist of some things that you need to be sure to consider before walking out the door. Oftentimes, once you inform Human Resources or your manager of your intent to resign, certain organizations will go ahead and accept your resignation on the spot. Depending on what your current policies are, be prepared for that in addition to the realization that your relationship will likely change within the time period that you give your notice and the time that you actually depart.

Review and Update Your Job Description

While you still have full access, the first thing you must do is review your job description: adjust it with any additional responsibilities that you've picked up or any additional task or projects that you've taken on that you feel have permanently evolved into part the role. Currently, you are the only subject matter expert on your current job description; therefore, you have an opportunity to leave your organization with a more realistic perspective of the job requirements than when you began. This will also be a great refresher for what's going to go in to updating your resume because if you remember what you were asked to do initially, compared to what you actually accomplished, you'll have a head start on creating a complete and accurate record of your job performance as you prepare your resume to submit to the next hiring manager.

Test Your Network

Secondly, begin to test your network. Become more present and active on social media, especially sites like LinkedIn. Follow companies that you respect and may become interested in working for, and begin to see what factors have changed in the industry and the environment since you were hired for your present job. Examine current hiring trends for changes in technology and what employers are asking for in recent job postings. Are there any terms that the companies are using to describe certain functions? Are they asking for experiences that previously were not necessarily on the forefront of many job descriptions and applications? Ensure that you've got a consistent pulse on where your industry is compared to where it was when you entered your current position. Depending on how long you've been in your current job, this may be a relatively quick assignment. But, if you've been in an organization for several years given the rate of rapid technology upgrades and the changing of the job market, it would be good to spend a little bit of time getting familiar with what it's like to be out there in the job market before actually entering it.

Evaluate Your Finances

Third, and this is going to be a more personal one for every individual, is for you to take some time to review your financial state. Consider that if you walked into your office today and offered your two weeks' notice and the manager responded, "You know what, I appreciate that but it's fine. Go ahead and collect your things. We'll terminate our employer-employee relationship at this particular time." Twenty minutes later, you're driving out of the parking lot. If that were the case, how much money would you realistically have access to in order to sustain your current lifestyle without employment? How long could you go without a job? Consider your current retirement plans and if you have access to money there that you could withdraw, keeping in mind the penalties associated with doing so. Conduct a thorough review including a new budget without the income to ensure that you've got a 360 degree understanding of what life would be like without the income from your current job as well as how long that could reasonably last.

It's important to set up a time with your Human Resources or Benefits Manager to try and understand exactly what benefit packages you have available. What is the process for transferring any pension or retirement accounts from one company to another or managing those on your own? How much of the company's money has been vested in your individual IRA? Well, the amount that you're used to seeing on a quarterly basis change if you've not met a certain time threshold.

Understand Your Benefits

Next, you should consider your benefits. What about COBRA? Will you have access to extending any current health coverage? What was the agreement when you signed-on, and is the company prepared to ensure policies are in place to provide some continuity for any benefits package that you have been offered? If you have to enter the healthcare marketplace to purchase healthcare coverage, what will that process look like and what will be the financial commitment in doing so? Understanding your benefits outlook, especially if you've got family members or dependents that are used to benefiting from your employer-sponsored plan, will be critical in understanding your entire financial picture and how long you can realistically sustain your current lifestyle before securing another job.

FYI

Per the United States Department of Labor, The Consolidated Omnibus Budget Reconciliation Act (COBRA) gives workers and their families who lose their health benefits the right to choose to continue group health benefits provided by their group health plan for limited periods of time under certain circumstances such as voluntary or involuntary job loss, reduction in the hours worked, transition between jobs, death, divorce, and other life events. Qualified individuals may be required to pay the entire premium for coverage up to 102 percent of the cost to the plan.

Review Company Policies on Resignation

At some point, you must prepare to actually have the conversation with your boss and with the decision-making process in place to help you determine how you want to go out, answering the question "What is the final piece of your reputation that employees and co-workers will remember about your departure?". It would be advised to have a face-to-face conversation with your boss before you actually submit a written letter of resignation. Before you schedule the meeting, ensure that you consult the organization's policies and procedures for how much notice it expects you to actually provide. It will probably also list who, besides your direct supervisor, you need to visit with to schedule an exit interview or any other formalities. The generally accepted standard for departure notice is going to be two weeks, but some jobs require a month or more with some jobs even requiring up to 90 days. As an administrative and legal officer in the Marine Corps, I actually had a young PFC try and submit a two-weeks-notice letter. I appreciated his professionalism but quickly had our department Gunnery Sergeant remind him that this was one business that didn't work quite that way. Once again, don't be surprised if, depending on the nature of your business, you're asked to leave a business immediately to avoid compromising any confidential or proprietary information.

Plan the Conversation

Oftentimes, family businesses and some companies, where more personal relationships are developed, will consider your departure an insult, which can be the result of not giving them time to truly process anything that you may have said (which is where a resignation letter will come into play and be a little bit more important). Truthfully, I'm guilty of not properly allowing for processing of a departure by management, as I had one particular job that I had actively disengaged from at least 60 days before I actually departed. I began to slowly take my belongings home from my office as I neared the time that I knew I was going to have to have that difficult conversation. Every day that I completed a normal workday and remained committed to the fact that I was going to leave, I took something else home from the office. This went on until, finally, the time arrived for me to have the conversation with the boss, and my office had been completely cleaned out for approximately two weeks without him noticing that there was ever anything different. Now, that should give you some perspective to the boss' level of engagement into my work-a-day world and the job that I was doing, but it should also tell you that it was weighing on my mind heavily, and I had begun to disengage from the organization long before I had the moral courage to have the crucial conversation. I would not recommend that to anybody contemplating departing an organization because it doesn't contribute to sustaining a healthy relationship.

For the initial notification conversation, ask your manager for a time that you could have his undivided attention for a five-to-ten-minute conversation. When that time arrives, the first thing to do is just tell your boss right up front that you're leaving. Get straight to the point and save some small talk and any formalities as it would be appropriate to just say, "I am here to offer my resignation effective immediately" (or effective two weeks from this date). Getting right to the point will signal that you're serious about the decision and will escalate your conversation's importance when compared to any previous that you may have had in the same office or setting. The emotional context of an employee leaving will quickly grab the manager's attention, especially if he is disengaged and expecting a routine discussion. I used to have conversations with the boss where it wasn't uncommon for him to make eye contact only two or three times throughout the meeting, as he was normally sending an email or screening phone calls or knocks at the door. Saying something as abrupt as, "I offer my resignation" will certainly give cause for the undivided attention of the boss to be directed to you if it were not previously committed. Keep the conversation short and to the point, as they'll need time to digest it. Make sure that it's a professional and not personal conversation, even if the relationship is one that's been founded on a more personal platform, for this is a time where you keep the direction strictly focused on where you're headed and do not venture outside of the conversation's intent. Speak positively (as best you can), especially when you get into the point to describe why you're leaving. You don't want this to be the time that you set out to air your dirty laundry, unless you believe that this is the only opportunity you'll have to do so. Let the boss know in so many words that you recognize the need to move on with your career, and you believe that the appropriate next step is to depart the current organization. If the boss presses a little bit further and asks you the direct question, "Why are you leaving?", or "I know I'm going to get asked. Lots of people are going to want to know, so what should I tell them?", be mindful to keep it positive as you venture into more sensitive territory. This is the time where you have control of the message surrounding your departure. Your boss may press further if it's perceived that there is probably more to the conversation and say, "All right, tell me what's really going on." If there are aspects about the company culture that you wish to disclose, then this is the time to do so. If your primary issue with the organization is one that is stemming from the leadership or management structure (perhaps even the person sitting in front of you), then don't hesitate to bring it up in this juncture; *however*, try to do so in a calm and objective manner as not to inject too much emotion which could detract from the message. You may be asked as to where you're going. Once again, be familiar with your organization's policies, especially if there's any sort of non-compete clause before you answer the question, as this may affect the outcome of how long you stay with the company.

Remain Gratuitous

Always try to circle the conversation back to some level of appreciation. Express your appreciation for past training, past experiences you've had with the organization, the relationships that you've formed, and above all, the opportunity the manager gave you to do so, reminding the manager that this wasn't an easy decision. Even if you're extremely angry and unhappy, find something positive to say. Even if it's one that's been weighing on your mind for quite some time, you've put a lot of thought into it, and there's been some levels of it that have been difficult. Let your manager know that you've learned a lot and what parts of the organization that you've enjoyed (if any), as you want to close the conversation on a somewhat positive note. At the end of the day, you don't want to burn any bridges because you're now at the point in your career where you want to prepare to start building bridges, therefore, the relationship may be helpful later.

Go For It!

Now, we've all seen scenarios in movies and otherwise where there's been the very dramatic departure from an organization, and, granted, you may be in a situation where there is no other way than driving your point home hard in your one opportunity. I can tell you that I've done them all in my career. I've offered the casual resignation letter. I've had the conversation with a complacent boss who had also reached the conclusion that it was time to develop an exit strategy between organization and myself (but he had failed to notice that my office had been completely cleaned out for the two weeks prior to that conversation). I've also done the dramatic exit in the middle of a Board of Directors' meeting because the company culture had become so toxic that it was purely unbearable. It had weighed on my mind for quite some time, but I had failed the organization by not letting anybody know until it was immediately before.

My situation is a little different because I was simultaneously being considered for a promotion to the chief executive position of the organization. From a lot of people's perspective, I was the right guy at the right time to move into the seat and "right the ship". What was under the surface, according to the iceberg metaphor, was all of the toxic elements of the organization that had really started to take a toll on me personally and professionally. In the information that we discussed early here, 90% of the organization can be defined as toxic or flawed, and it would have been unhealthy and a poor leadership decision on my part to remain in the organization any longer. I was talking the night before the Board of Directors' meeting with a very close friend and mentor of mine and was sharing my thoughts and concern for the organization. I explained that I couldn't in good consciousness stay with the company any longer because the culture had become too toxic. My mentor's comment to me is one that I will never forget. He said, "All right, I get it. But if you're going to go out, you better come in there tomorrow with both guns blazin' and not leave anything on the table." Which is exactly what I did. As I replay the scene in my mind, it plays out like the "Scarface quit his job" scene with Julio in the movie *Half Baked*. As I walked through the door in the middle of a meeting, I threw down the most audacious verbal pipe bomb of word vomit that I would imagine and that I'm sure the Board of Directors have ever heard. I talked about the poor hiring processes the company had allowed. I talked about the micromanagement from the Board to the organizational employees. I vented about the fraternization with volunteer representatives. I discussed the mismanaged and inappropriate vendor relationships that were creating "contracted inefficiency" into our processes. I mentioned a few other observations that I'd seen in my tenure that I thought was wrong with the organization and that ultimately led to my departure, but I honestly cannot remember it all. I spewed all of my discontent in about ten minutes. The fact that I can't remember what I said is a problem because that means they probably don't remember it either. In hindsight, I would absolutely recommend not quitting in that manner because, while it was very emotional and extremely passionate and overly heated for a moment, within 12 hours, I would venture to say that not one of them could tell you half of the things that I said. It was too abrupt, too quick, and in their minds probably seemed irrational, even though I had contemplated the event for quite some time. Giving your organization the dramatic "F-you" themed speech will feel great...for a minute. It may even feel good as you're driving home blasting Taylor Swift's "We Are Never Ever Getting Back Together" for a little while. But as I mentioned before, no one often remembers how you enter and organization, but they are likely to remember the manner in which you depart.

The Resignation Letter

The professional thing to do and the best thing for the organization's sake is to capture all of your reasoning for departing in more of a traditional and conventional resignation letter. The resignation letter is one of the more professional ways to resign in terms of easing transition for the organization, and if constructed in the right way, will help maintain a positive relationship with the employer, even if at the time you don't believe that there's anything beneficial about doing so. The resignation letter should be simple, brief, and focused. Resist the temptation of just leaving the resignation letter on somebody's desk. If you have access to the building on a Sunday afternoon, don't be the employee who comes in and leaves the letter for your boss to find first thing Monday morning after you've already cleaned out your desk. Like your notification conversation, the letter should be as positive as it possibly can under the circumstances. You made the decision to move on, so don't bother criticizing your employer or your current job, at least not in this particular manner. The contents of your letter are going to sustain for quite some time, longer than anything you say verbally. They will become part of your permanent employee record in all likely circumstances and will, as previously mentioned, contribute to your legacy.

As far as the construct of your resignation letter goes, once again, be up front and tell your superiors not only that you're leaving but also when your resignation is effective. Secondly, be gracious for the opportunity that you've had during your employment. If nothing else, you head right to the point and may conclude with some level of gratitude. Try to avoid emailing (and especially text messaging) your resignation notification, as there's something professional to be said about a formal letter that's obviously been given some thought and constructed with poise and professionalism.

Under some circumstances, like a cross country move or a decision to focus on starting a family, it may not be necessary to talk in detail about why you're resigning. But, if you're going to cite an unbearable company culture as your rationale for departing, then you will do the organization no better service than explaining in detail where the organization is failing its employees ("both guns blazin'", remember?). Depending on your current level of disengagement, at this point you may feel that you owe your employers nothing more than adherence to company policy. Advise them of that as well in the form of short, concise, paragraphs letting them know that you no longer intend to contribute to the organizational mission. Most resignation letters are not going to be more than one typed page; it doesn't need to be a dissertation or even a Master's thesis. Just get to the point, do not leave any questions unanswered in terms of your committed adherence to company policy, and prepare to make your exit.

Resignation letter organization should be very straightforward as there are many templates that you can find online, but the basic format is as follows:

Use a header with your and the employer's contact information. Insert the date. Have a salutation that addresses the letter to your manager and maybe a courtesy copy to Human Resources being mindful to using everyone's formal titles.

In the first paragraph, state that you're resigning and include the date that your resignation will be effective Once again, be upfront, to the point, and clear. Check your contract, if you have one, as well as company policies to see how much notice you should give and ensure that the date that you put in the correspondence is compliant with that policy.

If you would like to give some detail about your decision to leave, although this is not necessary, then do so in the second paragraph. If you choose to say why you're leaving, be as positive as possible when you describe it. Talk about what you want out of your career, where you're headed in terms of the next step in support of what you want out of your career, and not necessarily all of the aspects that you disliked about your current position.

The third paragraph is where you may discuss your willingness to help in a transition. Let them know that you're available during the transition time line to assist in any new employee training or ensuring that you set the organization up for success while they search for your replacement.

The fourth paragraph is where you can request a reference letter from your manager or Human Resources Department. In this way, you will have a clearly written record of a reference document that you can take with you. You may also offer to write letters of recommendation or endorsements for fellow employees.

In the final paragraph, thank management for the opportunity to work for the organization. If you had a particularly good experience, then make sure that you mention that specifically. You can go into a little bit more detail about what you personally appreciated about the job, the people you worked with, the projects you contributed to, which will at least show that you are at least making the effort to leave in a somewhat positive manner.

Finally, close with a formal sign off such as "sincerely" or "respectfully" with a signature followed by your typed name. Short, concise, to the point, nothing overly dramatic. This is just a token of professionalism and adherence with company policy in letting them know that you're on your way out.

The following pages include examples of both inappropriate and appropriate versions of employee resignation letters.

An inappropriate resignation letter may look like this:

Date

Dear Bryan,

I am writing to inform you of my resignation. My last day was pretty much last Friday. Since then, I've been using company time and resources to update my Pinterest and to find a better job.

Thankfully, I was offered a fantastic opportunity at our competitor yesterday, and I start Monday (with a promotion and salary increase).

Too bad I never signed the non-compete agreement, Sucka!

Peace and Love,

Lauren

An appropriate resignation letter could look something like the following:

Mike Jones Executive Director
1980 KnowyourRole Blvd.
Stamford, CT, 06902

January 9th, 2017

Ray Peterson, Chairman of the Board
Smackdown Hotels, Inc.
1980 KnowyourRole Blvd.
Stamford, CT, 06902

Cc: Human Resources, for file

Mr. Chairman:

I am writing to announce my resignation from Smackdown Hotels, Inc., effective at the close of business on 23 January 2017.

This was not an easy decision for me to make. The past five years have been very rewarding. I've enjoyed working with you and working with a very successful team dedicated to providing top-tier customer service and hospitality to our guests. I am departing to focus more of my time and efforts on my developing energy drink proprietorship, which is where I hope to establish as an international brand within the next year.

Throughout the course of my next two weeks, I look forward to the opportunity to assist in the transition in any way that I can, as I wish to set the organization up for success.

If possible, I would greatly appreciate a letter of recommendation for my personal employment files, which may be beneficial to me in the future. I will gladly be authoring several for employees with whom I have worked during my time here.

Thank you again for your leadership, and I hope we can keep in touch in the future.

Sincerely,

Signature (hard copy letter)

Mike Jones

Inform Your Coworkers

Once your letter has been constructed, the next process that you'll undergo is finalizing the exit strategy. The environment will be awkward between the time that you resign and the time that you actually leave, but as your exit strategy is going to contribute to your overall organizational representation, have things prepared to walk out the door when you make that announcement. Think about the relationships that you want to preserve, and consider the feelings of your co-workers and your customers. When considering how they perceive their relationships with you, take time to talk to them about your departure. Don't be overly gloating about your new opportunity, if one exists; realize instead that this is the time to ensure that the organization and the people that you work with are set up for success. Remain humble and courteous, and avoid being patronizing in all conversations that surround your leaving. If your employer allows it, you may wish to send out an email to all of your coworkers and let them know collectively that you're leaving your job. This will allow you to fully control the message that surrounds your departure and to try to head off any rumors or circumstantial assumptions. This would be preferred to your simply not showing up one day.

A sample mass e-mail to your coworkers could look as follows:

From: Jones, Michael A.
To: ALL TEAM MEMBERS
Subject: Mike Jones Update

To my fellow employees, colleagues, and friends:

As some of you may have heard, I am leaving the organization two weeks from today.

This was not an easy decision, as I have thoroughly enjoyed my time here. More than the work, I have enjoyed working alongside you all.

The time has come, though, to pursue new ventures in my life and career as I follow a dream to own my own business that I've had for quite some time.

I hope to stay in touch with you all. Please, know that I can be reached at my personal email address: mike.jones@gmail281.com.

Thank you all again, Mike

Transition Logistics

On your last day, you may have the opportunity to conduct an exit interview. At this time, appropriate management personnel will provide you with information regarding your final pay and benefits and things that you should have already done some research on at this point. As your last day approaches, you may be asked to have a more formal conversation with multiple people in terms of your transition. You'll have to turn in all of your company access cards and ID cards; your corporate credit cards, keys, tools, company equipment. You'll also have the opportunity to answer some questions that may be standard from corporate but maybe also specific to your departure.

While that first conversation with your manager is not the time to necessarily air your dirty laundry, this may be the time to do so because this will be a very private, closed-door conversation with your manager and Human Resources personnel. This is where you'll thank the people who have given you support, say goodbye and shake hands with your boss and the Human Resources Manager, and close the exit interview conversation in a particularly professional manner.

Throughout your two-week period, make sure that you save documentation that is not proprietary to the organization that could contribute to your overall work result portfolio. You'll want to take things with you from job to job that's a specific testament to your work abilities and experiences.

In addition, ensure that before you turn in all equipment that you've taken the opportunity to save anything personal on a separate device or email it to your personal address. This was problematic for me in a previous position because I had not done my due diligence in having an effective exit strategy or even given the professional courtesy of two weeks' notice. After dropping my dramatic pipe bomb exit to the Board of Directors, I had about eight hours to get all of my personal belongings together, do a complete turnover, and exit the organization. My organization had used Google Drive for all of our document and data storage, which is what I also personally used. At some point, I had lost the line of personal information and company information in the consolidation of my files within one central Google Drive location. On my way out, my intent was to delete anything personal that may have been accessed on a company device so as to prevent any of my personal documentation ending up the property of the organization. Now, one lesson that anybody who has ever worked in a professional setting will be able to tell you (and most of us know): you should never mix personal and business on the same device. As things get more streamlined and cloud-based, it's going to be more difficult to maintain that separation; however, that separation is going to be increasingly important in safely segregating your personal and professional activities. When I initiated my delete, I inadvertently deleted every file belonging to both the organization and my personal drive from the cloud in its entirety. So, not only did the organization lose data, but my many years of personal documents and programs were deleted as well, creating quite an awkward moment for everybody involved. With more detailed planning, a little bit more professionalism, and an overall stronger exit strategy, the awkwardness and subsequent document recovery could have been avoided.

It Doesn't Have to be Depressing!

As you're in the middle of physically transitioning out of your office, it can be a very emotional time ranging from happiness, anger, relief, depression, and everything in between. Your commitment to escaping a toxic environment in pursuit of a brighter and more rewarding workplace is a big step towards a more engaging employee experience and should be celebrated! To help you look past some of the anxiety that can often accompany a career transition, here is a list of the top ten songs for cleaning out your office, turning in your badge, and rocking out of the parking lot one last time.

The Top Ten "Quit Your Job" Anthems:

10.) "Roar", Katy Perry, Capitol Records, 2013
9.) "My Way", Limp Bizkit, Interscope, 2001

8.) "Wrecking Ball", Miley Cyrus, RCA, 2013

7.) "Deuces", Chris Brown, Jive, 2010

6.) ["This Job] Better Have My Money", Rhianna, Roc Nation, 2015

5.) "Stronger", Kanye West, Roc-A-Fella, 2007

4.) "Movin' Out", Billy Joel, Columbia, 1977

3.) "We Are Never Ever Getting Back Together", Taylor Swift, Big Machine, 2012

2.) "I Don't [Mess] With You", Big Sean, GOOD, 2014

1.) "Bye Bye Bye", N'Sync, Jive, 2000

Departing Thoughts

The only things that you will leave behind as you walk out the door for the last time are the results that you've created and the manner in which you departed. Considering all facets about the organization, the highs, the lows, the emotional ups and downs, the toxic elements and the shortcomings, the only thing that you'll truly be able to take with you and preserve for as long as you make the effort to do so is the relationships with the individuals. As you leave behind friends and colleagues, ensure that the message you leave is one of positivity and willingness to continue your professional relationship in some form or fashion, hoping that you'll cross paths again. Leaving an organization can be a complicated and emotional process, but when due diligence is done in preparation and formulation of an exit strategy, it can be accomplished in a seamless and professional manner.

Chapter Nine
Don't Settle Down, Step Up.

Take Home Message:

- If there is any time between quitting your last job and starting your new one, enjoy the career detoxification cycle: Rest, Repair, Reflect, Refocus, Reclaim.

- Plan ahead for your first impression at the new workplace by arriving early and making a focused effort on observing how procedure are done; ask questions and take notes

- Mentorship in a new role will be key. If the company doesn't provide one, find one

- Develop open lines of communication with your manager, especially when it comes to performance; build the same communication infrastructure with your coworkers

- Find your place in the culture through building relationships; don't force it

---

Fifteen years ago, news personality Megyn Kelly was working aggressively as a high paid attorney and was married to a physician.

"On paper, I felt that I was succeeding," says Kelly, who would watch *Oprah* reruns when she came home from working 18-hour days in Chicago, NYC, and Baltimore. But according to her memoir, *Settle for More*, she says she was not happy or fulfilled. One night, as she was watching Dr. Phil McGraw as a guest on Oprah Winfrey's show, "Dr. Phil said something that I would never forget and that would change my life forever: 'The only difference between you and someone you envy is you settled for less,'" Kelly recalls. "It hit me like a lightning bolt. I resolved right then and there in that moment that I could settle for more."

Truthfully, I never realized how dissatisfied I was in my previous job until I finished Megyn Kelly's book and saw how truly happy and fulfilled she had become after committing her life to "settling for more." I knew that the organization had problems; I realized that there were elements of the company culture that were toxic, but I never resolved as to what I would do about it until I'd read the story of someone who had found a way out of toxicity and into happiness. The book was refreshing to read because it detailed the story of someone who appeared on camera to have everything together, basically everything that the rest of us would aspire to attain. However, through her vulnerable recounting of her life's events, it became apparently clear that no one is immune to ending up in a situation of working every day for a job that she hates, and everyone has the ability to step outside of what's comfortable and pursue what's truly desired both personally and professionally.

Moving On

After all of the thought and anxiety that has transpired over making the decision to leave a job that has created depression and discontent, the task at hand is to become determined not to repeat the same cycles of your professional past. Instead of settling downward towards what is easiest, and perhaps most convenient in terms of job availability, commit to stepping up toward something greater in terms of professional challenge and satisfaction.

While there are hundreds of ways of applying for new jobs with each internet posting generating a flood of indiscriminant and unqualified applicants, it's hard enough to land a job that you are often over-qualified for as it is. So, the pursuit of something slightly outside of your comfort zone may not be as enticing as playing it safely. But think of it this way, there was probably nothing safe about making the decision to leave, and if after all of the potential problem areas and backfires that come with making the decision to leave a position still steers you out the door, then it makes even less sense to step back toward familiarity as opposed to stepping up toward happiness. In the words of Rocky Balboa as he's standing toe to toe with Clubber Lang in *Rocky III*, "Go for it." Regardless of the job you're moving into, one thing that's certain is that you don't want to repeat the same toxic cycle in less than a year - it's too time consuming and too stressful! So, in pursuit of your ultimate career success, here are some things to keep in mind regarding the transition and making your home in your new job a pleasant one.

A Fresh Start

As you've landed your next job and are excited about beginning the next stage of your career, enjoy all of the resurfacing feelings and enthusiasm that you had as you began your last job. You're probably excited as you're thinking about the new projects and relationships as well as the new components that you'll soon develop to your body of work as a professional. After you've accepted the job offer and you've decided on a start date and a compensation, it would be a good idea to maintain some level of contact with your new employer. Start to work on projects that you know will fall into your purview, gain information about the organization, and ask the questions that will ensure that when you walk through the door you're prepared to hit the ground running. After their initial drug screening and background check and anything else they have in their hiring process, ask for any paperwork from human resources to guarantee that as much of the administrative requirements that can be done prior to your arrival are completed so that you can quickly begin focusing on your contributions.

If you have any time between the conclusion of your previous job and the beginning of your next one, enjoy it. Spend some time with your family and organize your life a little bit. Recharge your batteries. Get some rest, and remember what exactly it is that you want out of this next career venture. Spend time learning new things and reading books for enjoyment. Ensure that you've become familiar with what's changed in the workplace between the last time that you began a new job and this one.

The Employee Cultural Detoxification Cycle

Whenever I've had some time between one job and another, I always used it as a period when I can go to the gym at a reasonable hour, perhaps eight or nine o'clock in the morning as opposed to four thirty or five. I want to be sure that I take some time to get healthy again. Use your time off to rejuvenate your mind and rest your body. The cycle of cultural detoxification can be defined in five stages: Rest (your body and your mind), Repair (the mental and physical aspects that may have been damaged from the last job, Reflect (on why you left), Refocus (on what you want from your next position), and Reclaim (your place of professional prominence in the workplace.

One component of toxic workplaces is oftentimes that employees will find themselves working long hours, which leads to their unhappiness and departure. Now that you've got some time to relax and detox a little bit, ensure that you're investing in your health to rejuvenate your mind and your body as you begin to start your next adventure. Rest your muscles and your mind as part of part of your motive to remove any of the residual toxins from your recent organization.

There's a million articles on how to make a great first impression as you return to work. There are some steps that are inherent in making a great start that people in any preparatory stage for a new career will already know such as being mindful that you show up at least 15 minutes early. You'll want to make sure that you have access to the building at normal times, that you know where you're going and who to talk to, and that you have your new commute planned out. When you accepted the job, Human resources probably told you about the dress code, but if you're not sure, then make sure that you choose on the more conservative side. You want to be memorable on your first day but not necessarily for how you look. When you get to the office, ensure that you're overly professional even if your office seems a little bit more casual. Err on the side of professionalism until you're sure that you get everybody figured out. If you have some people from your professional network already in the environment, they'll be invaluable in facilitating your smooth arrival and transition into your new team.

Your goal is not just trying to get to know everybody, as you're trying to let people get to know you. Even if it's uncomfortable, there's no better time than on your first day at a new job to channel your inner extrovert. Try and say hi to everybody who passes your desk, and introduce yourself even though it may not be your forte, and you be a little bit uncomfortable. Visit with people about their role with the organization, and try to learn as many names as you can, as opposed to just a title. Remember, it's about relationships, and not necessarily the organizational chart. If your workday is scheduled to end at five or six, stay a little longer. Get the feel for how everybody perceived his role in the office. Who stays the latest, and who are the centers of gravity in terms of personnel? Who does most everybody go and talk to when they have a question? Who are the new influencers in terms of the organization and what people view as the way to get things done?

It's easy to understand that you may have a few uncertainties as you enter into the new environment, so in order to get there a little bit earlier, make sure that you wake up a bit earlier. Ensure that you received a good night's sleep so that you may start your day slightly earlier than normal. If you're somebody who likes to hit the snooze button, maybe set your alarm 30 minutes earlier so you can be sure that you get at least three snoozes in. Plan to have your coffee in hand and be walking out the door in plenty of time to get you to your new workplace.

Make It Your Own

Starting a new job is going to feel like you're moving into a new house. I remember that the home buying process that started many months before I was actually ready to start looking at properties. I researched and knew what I liked and what I didn't. I knew what I wanted and expected in terms of community growth. I talked to agents and found one whom I liked and could trust to guide the process. I felt like I had done everything possible to get ready for the actual time that an offer was made, a deal was done, and I was ready to start moving in. There's nothing quite like moving into a new house or apartment and really making it your own, especially after coming from a less-than-desirable environment. In order to replicate that feeling, structure your approach to the workplace the same way. If you're familiar to some degree with the layout of your workspace, prepare to move in and make it your own. Set up your space as if you're setting up your new house. It isn't going to feel like yours until your boxes are unpacked, your pictures are on the wall, and you begin to feel that it's not new at all.

A quick way to begin to feel like part of the team is to set up your e-mail signature. Make sure that people are familiar with your name and your title. Don't hesitate to send something out to let people know that you've arrived and what you do there. Get rid of all of the old voicemail greeting recordings on your desk phone and company cell phone. Ensure that people know your extension and when they call to expect to talk to coworkers in your department. If they don't get you via interoffice phone, they'll at least get a new greeting letting them know who you are.

Take the time to observe how your colleagues personalize their own work spaces and communication devices. Listen to their voicemails when you call. Ask them if the company has any policies regarding any standard greetings that you're expected to use, and take a tour around to see how many personal effects they have on their desks. You don't want to go overboard, but you do want to ensure that you fit right in with the normal standards of personalization in the general office space.

Mingle with Others

Try to make some time to schedule an offsite lunch with somebody. If your office is one that provides a cafeteria or something where most employees usually get food, schedule some time to visit with somebody potentially out of the work environment. That's where you'll really begin to break that barrier and develop a closer relationship than what the routine office environment usually permits.

On any new employee's first day with my organization, I would schedule him with another manager or team member for an offsite lunch. Their initial level of comfort increases significantly with a more personal introductory event. Use this time to ask individuals some questions about their jobs, what they do; you know, things that aren't work-related. If you're in a new town, then you may ask how your fellow employees spend time on a weekend? What do you they do outside of the work for fun or recreation? You'll likely bond over the course of that offsite lunch, and if nothing else, you'll have a potential conversation starter for the next time that you get together.

Consider what may be going through the other employees' minds as you've just started there. They're wanting to gain some insight in to you in much the same way, so offer some information about yourself to give them a perspective to what you're bringing to the table and maybe why you were hired. Remind them subtly of the skill sets that you'll bring to the team. Try not to overly brag about what you've accomplished as it may appear that you're trying to re-interview for a position as their friend or coworker. You've already got the job; that box is checked. Now, you're genuinely focused on building relationships, so you want to share just enough to let your coworkers know that there's more to you than the job description and requirements.

Whether this is your second position or your 20th, the first few days on the job are going to be a little bit intimidating. The remainder of the chapter is dedicated to presenting some "food for thought" for the new employee to consider after he has checked in and is beginning to contribute.

It will be important not to over commit yourself in an attempt to prove your worth. Be cautious and tactical, ensuring that your schedule is balanced and that you have plenty of time to learn the ropes around the new environment. You don't want to appear that you have too much to do or that you're overwhelmed. So, resist the urge to try and prove yourself through constant volunteerism for committees and projects. Pace yourself in terms of what you take on outside of your initial functions as you begin to learn the actual job requirements and your manager's expectations.

Be sure that you ask enough questions of everybody with whom you come into contact. If you have a standing meeting with your supervisor, then go prepared with a list of things that you need and want to know about the work environment. Ask your coworkers at formal or informal settings about policies and procedures within the organization. My first day on my very first job in the Marine Corps, I walked into my executive officer's office, and I will never forget the piece of advice that he gave me. He said, "Welcome to the fleet. I understand that you will have questions. Ask them. Don't ever hesitate to come in this office and ask something that you're unsure of. Our job is to make sure that you're successful."

I've taken that piece of advice and practice into every subsequent job, whether it was offered or not, and as I've begun to manage employees of my own, I share the same thought with them all on their first day. Ask questions early and often to avoid missing something that will potentially be beneficial down the road. As you attend meetings, don't be afraid to participate being ever mindful that you want to reinforce to your boss and everybody else the reason that you were hired. You won't know everything and you shouldn't act like you do, so the vulnerability of asking questions when you don't know something will contribute to building trust with both your coworkers and superiors.

Take Copious Notes

Even if it's not your style, take as many notes as you can about what you learn. Save them in a way that you may reference them for years. I've got binders from place to place that I've worked that I reference every time I'm beginning a new position. Past workplace history serves as a good refresher to know how organizations compare and what knowledge you can bring into a new workplace that may benefit the organization. Absorb everything that you possibly can and commit to writing it down. As your brain is absorbing a large amount of new information, there's going to be some information that is dropped and some information that is missed. Remaining diligent in taking notes and making a point to circle back when the time and place is conducive to following up will reduce the missing of details due to information overload.

In your first couple of weeks, you'll begin to feel your company's culture by the way that it communicates, its values, the teammates, the projects, the problems, the politics, the company-wide and departmental goals that are in place. What you'll feel in terms of the culture will indicate how you're expected to contribute, and how you anticipate your skill set will lend you to fitting in. Keeping an open and objective mind for gaps, you should perceive how your new company expresses value to its employees.

Managing Your New Workplace Expectations

During the onboarding process, you should become familiar with what the company offers in terms of benefits and professional development. Start to think about those aspects that interest you in terms of where you want to go with your position in the organization without seeming too eager to take on something new until you (as well as your coworkers and managers) are fully comfortable with your performance in your new position.

To some degree, every company wants the same thing. They wouldn't have hired you if they didn't want you to be successful. It's inherent that your success is going to be dependent upon learning and understanding new processes, new people, new projects, and new expectations. Try not to be an employee always comparing things to the way things were done at your last job because, after all, you left your last job for a reason. As you're in a business that will hopefully appreciate creativity and innovation, ask a question such as "What if we did it like this?" If you have a skill or ability that you know you can bring to the team that they're not currently possessing or exhibiting, don't hesitate to step up and step into your role and contribute help and some guidance, skill sets which will move the organization forward.

If you're feeling things out before you take on some projects, then you may experience that you've got some downtime. As you're waiting maybe for your first task or to fully get up to speed on what was being done before, you may take this opportunity to assist in other areas of the business. Without overstepping or seeming like you're unsure of what your actual responsibilities are, don't hesitate to reach out and offer to help your colleagues or coworkers in the spirit of developing relationships.

Mentorship- A Must Have!

One thing that you'll want to ensure that you do, and I can't emphasize enough, is find a mentor. One of the weakest organizations that I worked with in terms of ability to be strategic and agile in the way that they developed as a business, did in fact have one element that was probably the most beneficial in terms of my personal development - they assigned me a mentor. I was fortunate enough to work with the CFO (who I might add is one of the most genuinely authentic people whom I've ever had the privilege of working with) in a mentor/mentee capacity. He mentored me not necessarily in elements of my job, as he was an accountant as the chief financial officer, and I was in human resources, and there were things about employment laws, employee relations, and compensation and benefits that he couldn't help me with. But, the things that he could tell me were the things that I wasn't going to find in any policy manual or employee handbook with this organization because he gave me firsthand insight into the company's practices and culture. In terms of what the company intended to accomplish in terms of goals and productivity, well there was no better example throughout the organization than my relationship with this particular colleague.

FYI

Mentoring is one of the oldest forms of influence and knowledge sharing. It started with the Ancient Greeks, as Mentor was Odysseus' trusted counselor and advisor. Mentoring is when one individual actively and willingly passes their knowledge and wisdom to another person. A mentor is an individual that is usually older, but always more experienced, who helps and guides another individual's development. This guidance is done without the expectation of personal or monetary gain on the mentor's part. Mentors can be friends, relatives, coworkers, teachers, supervisors, etc.

If the organization that you've became a part of does not have a formal mentorship program, then make a commitment to find and create one. Finding a seasoned veteran who can share with you the joys and discomforts of working in the organization from a firsthand, been-there-done-that perspective, will prove invaluable to your ability to fit in to your new culture.

You should avoid relying on the mentor to do things for you professionally, and you should also be sensitive to the fact that the mentor is taking time out of his job requirements to share information and experiences with you. Respect the time that you agree to without asking for more or creating the perception that they're a crutch. My mentor was generous enough to give me one hour per week, every week, and I tried to respect that in the sense of not making repeated visits to his office outside of that schedule. If your mentor is gracious enough to give up time on his schedule, try and respect that as much as possible without overstepping.

Understand Feedback Mechanisms

Go out of your way to keep your boss informed of your progress. You don't want to constantly send emails updating them on routine tasks (because after all, they believed that you can do the job or you wouldn't be hired) but continue to keep them informed of projects that you've completed, especially if they've been directly tasked to you. Send emails at the end of every week capturing what you've accomplished to date and what you intend to start the next week. Phrase your sign-off in a way that you're asking for guidance, as in "Do you believe that I am working on the right things?" This will set a tone that you would like their feedback and insights at a regular interval and provide an open opportunity to advise you to go in a different direction if needed. One of an employee's greatest resources is the establishment of the reporting relationship and the installation of open lines of communication to ensure that he is going in the right direction and maintaining alignment with company and organizational goals and objectives. You're going to spend the next weeks, months, and maybe even years working with and for this person; therefore, ensuring that you've created a means to communicate back and forth honestly about your performance will contribute significantly to your success and your professional relationship development.

Develop Relationships

As you're meeting new people and continuing to work your way around the office, keep in mind that there's so much more to your professional life than just adding friends. You've got to make them. Understanding the company's culture and thriving within it will come from the strength and support of the professional network that you develop. Through intentional cultivation of new relationships, you will strengthen the network of trusted colleagues who will be resources for future projects, questions, and professional support. As you're continuing to meet and cultivate, keep in mind that one of the greatest compliments that you can pay to an individual is asking his opinion. Through networking and development of relationships, you immediately begin to foster a culture of teamwork, whether you realize its benefit right away. Company-provided training isn't going to have all the answers or keys to success. Some of the more important training will come from the way that you work with your new colleagues, as you remain sensitive to the fact that they're not the ones that are new and also have job requirements. They have maybe become comfortable in their jobs and positions and may not have a lot of time to dedicate to spending with you as you traverse the new environment. So, as you continue to work and remain respectful of their time, you'll want to ensure that you find ways to repay them for their efforts to some degree. This goes back to the offer to help mentally: if you have areas where you can contribute something to one of their projects or processes, then step up and offer to do so. Guarantee that you're willing to make this relationship of support a two-way street, contributing in any way that you can. After all, you're there not to necessarily do the job that you were hired for - nothing more, nothing less. You're there to be a contributing member of the organizational culture as the person that your fellow employees and coworkers want on their team, as opposed to the one who becomes a carrier of toxicity.

Remember Why You're Here

When unsure of how to proceed in a new situation, default to the faith that you have in the organizational mission and values. If you made the decision to work for a values-based organization, then look in the core values for the answers in times of uncertainty. When your values are clear, your choices are easy. When you're making choices that are rooted in your core values, and you're surrounded by a team that wants to support you (and you feel the same way), you will find that your job, and ultimately your career, are going to be much more personally and professionally fulfilling.

Through a carefully developed and deliberate approach to entering a new job, employees will find resolve in their decision to leaving the toxic environment of the past and stepping up to reclaim their place in an engaging and enjoyable culture.

Final Thoughts

This is the part where you clean out your desk while listening to "Closing Time" by Semisonic- an honorable mention on the list.

In today's society, it seems easier to find employees who are unhappy with their job than it is to find those who genuinely enjoy what they do. From immature and inexperienced leadership, unethical decision making, a commitment to top-down communication, and an overall lack of trust between employees and the organization, there are a variety of factors that contribute to a toxic company culture. The difference between a disgruntled employee surrounded by an organization filled with contempt and unmotivated coworkers and the highly engaged and satisfied employee is that the engaged employee decided that the toxicity was no longer worth the strenuous efforts.

The lack of a feeling of value, a sense of utility, achieved recognition, and unwavering trust will create a void in the employee's spirit who desires to contribute, as the organization is failing to meet his basic needs. The realization by the employee that he has become disappointed in the organization, that perhaps at one time promised him the world, will lead to a period of disengagement as a result of negative thoughts becoming actions.

The rise of the toxic culture and the dissatisfaction that accompanies it will only be combated by an emotionally intelligent employee who has taken the time to fully understand what he values in work and life as well as what he truly wants out of a workplace. To dig deeply into the limbic part of the brain and pull the reasons "why" people function the way that they do can be a humbling, yet insightful, experience; consequently, this is the first step in laying the foundation of an engaging employee experience.

Quitting a job can be an emotionally trying decision, and making the decision to do so is the most difficult part of the process because there is an incremental method for everything else that's required to make a smooth transition. In understanding the reasons why to leave a job, an emotionally intelligent employee must have the moral courage to take a journey through self-awareness, analysis of behaviors, and possibly the admission of the fact that "You know… maybe I'm the problem." Arming yourself with this understanding, coupled with the tools to further develop your self-management and social skills, will allow for the introspective preparation to move on to a healthier work environment and a fresh start. As an employee, don't ever regret making a decision to leave an organization in pursuit of an environment and culture that is more aligned with your personal values and career goals because you are the only subject matter expert on what you want in life.

Regardless of the circumstances surrounding your departure, commit to doing so with poise and professionalism, as many people will forget how you began your job, but they'll all remember how you'll leave it. Results will be forgotten, conversations will fade from your manager's memory, eventually your employee file will be permanently stored in an offsite facility, and the only things that will remain as part of your legacy are the relationships you've formed and sustained. If you're looking to make a personal investment in the future of your current organization, then by all means invest in its people. This investment will help form the basis of your professional network which will be beneficial for the remainder of your career.

Once again, congratulations on your decision to step away from a toxic culture, for as you will find, life's truthfully too short to be unhappy where you spend the majority of your waking hours. Stepping back from the emotion long enough to think about your resignation in terms of a process will serve you well in achieving a smooth and professional departure. As you re-enter the job market and pursue your next stop on your career road map, focus on aligning an organizational culture with your core values, and I assure you that an engaging and rewarding employee experience is just a resignation away. In the words of a true Human Resources Professional, "Best of luck in all of your future career endeavors."

Acknowledgements

I've never really found it easy to fully convey the gratitude I have for those who have supported my seemingly whimsical nature of changing from job to job in search of the "perfect" opportunity, but I'll give it a shot.

First and foremost, to the person who has put up with my big ideas and constant search for more, Jaclyn, thank you. From leaving school to return to work, having three jobs since then as well as the hours of time I took away from you to put this together, you're the living definition of patience. You're a constant reminder that I don't have to have the right job to be on the right track. You are my love and the reason I know that it's okay to refuse to settle for less. Whether this book sells four copies or four hundred, I still get to hang out with you; so good luck everybody else!

The Koch family, in particular my Dad and Papaw. If everyone could run a business like the two of you, there would never be any reason for books like this to exist or employees who constantly search for something more. Watching you two run your organizations has helped set the standards for what I expect in a workplace. Hearing things like, "If you're going to do something, do it right", and "Activity doesn't mean productivity" are templates that I have since used in leadership, and if more people could hear your advice it would surely transform their employee experience. Don't worry, I still remember that "Opinions are like assholes, everybody's got one" too.

Lauren, as the first person to read this manuscript of what seemed like a collection of complaints intertwined with a few facts, you helped put it together with your perfect balance of sincerity and sarcasm. I can't thank you enough for the commitment, attention to detail, and friendship that allowed you to answer the phone when you knew I'd be asking for a favor on the other end. You are the Trail Boss, the Five-Star General, and the only person who can always find a way to connect the dots. Bryan is not only my best friend but the only person I've ever met who can genuinely find the good in everyone. Bryan is the template for officership, leadership, and friendship. Thank God for the sponsorship program of the U.S.M.C that allowed you to pick me up from the airport in…oh, wait. You were playing golf that day and sent Jackson. Fair enough. In all seriousness, you possess the loyalty that so many people are hoping to find, and I can't thank you enough for everything.

Keen, Vinny, Bull, and Pumba: you gentlemen are not only the essence of "stugots", but you know how to run a world-class organization. If you don't see anything in this book that reminds you of yourselves, it's because I have never enjoyed a job more than when I worked with you all. The emotional intelligence of Keen, the decisive execution of objectives by Vinny, and Bull and Pumba creating a culture where everyone on the team wanted to give a little more in support of the mission was the epitome of an engaged company culture.

Tom, Aaron, and the Texas FFA Family: Without the Texas FFA, I wouldn't have had the courage to make the moves to pursue personal and professional excellence. My family taught me the values of respect, responsibility, and resiliency, and the Texas FFA provided the proving ground to learn why they're important. With almost ninety years of empowering young leaders to pursue more than they initially believe possible through their targeted development of positive life skills, and equipping them with a competitive edge in their drive toward career success, I am proud to have been a part of such a phenomenal organization. Of course, I wouldn't have experienced any of that if it weren't for the commitment demonstrated by my high school Agriculture-Science teacher, Mr. Perry. Thank you all for the patience, persistence, and perspiration you invested in providing me with the opportunity to grow and make a difference in the lives of others. Every employee who has ever worked for me is a reflection of the efforts of each of you, and what I gained through my Texas FFA experience. *(Note: If you're curious about some of the current initiatives and how the Texas FFA is continuing to give students a competitive edge in the workforce, please visit* MYTEXASFFA.ORG*)*

Randy and Lisa, starting out working with the two of you so many years ago really put the employee experience on a pedestal, and

I look forward to the time when we will work together again. Thank you for all of your support and guidance over the years.

Mark, as one of the most genuinely "good" people I've ever met, you are the best thing an employee could hope for in a mentor. You truly live to serve.

Cindi, you always said to let you know if there was anything you could do! Thank you for your faith in Bryan, Lauren, and me, and thank you for always showing up with a smile prepared to deliver excellence. Seeing you do so through the years has reinforced the principle that good enough isn't good enough if it can be better, and better isn't good enough if it can be best. You're the best, and for that I thank you. Even though I was never in your class, I can assure you that I have been your student.

Lastly, the commitment to take all of this information derived from my formal training and previous work experiences and put it into one reference was done in hopes of helping fellow employees. The motivation to do so has stemmed from the loss of a dear student of mine who seemed to live his life for the sole purpose of helping others. Johnny's personal mission statement was simple: "My purpose is to engage, encourage, and support those who are often left out, ignored, and neglected, so that everyone receives an equal opportunity to discover and utilize their potential." I'll do my best, as should all who are able, to #LiveLikeJohnny.

About the Author and Editing Team

John Tyler Koch is a native of Henderson, Texas and graduate of Texas A&M University where he studied Agricultural Leadership and Animal Science. In 2008, he joined the U.S. Marine Corps where he served as an Adjutant and Company Executive Officer while simultaneously completing his Master's Degree in Managerial Economics from the University of Oklahoma. Upon his end of active service in 2012, Tyler gained insight into the world of lean manufacturing and global supply chain management, which provided him with additional tools for his agile human resources management style. Tyler has spoken across the country on a variety of HR topics, in particular the evolution of the millennial employee, and specializes in the development of leadership training curriculum and helping companies foster a culture of employee engagement.

Lauren Emeigh Tye, the line editor for *Just Quit Already!*, is a leadership development and fundraising specialist from Tampa, Florida. Lauren earned her Bachelor's Degree in Psychology before obtaining her Master's degree in Communications. As a master-facilitator and seasoned personnel training specialist, Lauren has helped a countless number of organizations maximize their focus and productivity through targeted learning objectives and outcomes.

Cindi Somerville Rains served as the copy editor for *Just Quit Already!* and is a celebrated English and Language Arts professional, as well as the owner/director of The Protocol School of East Texas and Intensive Dance Company. In all initiatives, Cindi takes pride in helping her students achieve success through her detail-oriented approach to excellence. As a licensed etiquette consultant and expert technical writer, Cindi Rains' service as a professional consultant has led many students to success in the arenas of dance, pageantry, literary arts, and the art of the interview.